THE FORGIVENESS JOURNEY

THE FORGIVENESS JOURNEY

Transcend Your Hurt, Transform Your Life

NELLA COIRO

Sunrise Valley Publishers
Carmel, New York

Copyright © 2019 Nella Coiro. All rights reserved.

No part of this publication may be reproduced, distributed, or transmitted in any form or by any means, including photocopying, recording, or other electronic or mechanical methods, without the prior written permission of the copyright owner, except in the case of brief quotations embodied in critical reviews, and certain other noncommercial uses permitted by copyright law. Under no circumstances may any part of this book be photocopied for resale.

Library of Congress Control Number: 2019902394
ISBN 978-1-7339522-0-0 (paperback)
ISBN 978-1-7339522-1-7 (ebook)

This work is sold with the understanding, that neither the author, nor the publisher, is held responsible for any results accrued from the advice in this book.

Some names and identifying details have been changed to protect the privacy of individuals.

All of the chapter quotes and the poetry are written by the author.

Editing & Proofreading by Audrey Silverman.
Interior Design & Book Cover by Country Mouse Design.

Sunrise Valley Publishers
Carmel, New York
www.sunrisevalleypublishers.com

Author's website: www.nellacoiro.com

DEDICATION

*This book is dedicated to my husband, Kenny,
the love of my life, and my best friend.
I would not be the woman I am today,
without your endless love, patience, and support.*

*You have to admit,
it's been an interesting journey…*

CONTENTS

1. Introduction 13
2. What is Forgiveness? 21
3. The Science of Forgiveness 29
4. The Law of Attraction and Forgiveness 35
5. Are You Addicted to Your Victim Story? 45
6. Pain Killers and Emptiness Fillers 49
7. Self-Forgiveness & Taming Your Inner Critic 61
8. The Forgiveness Steps 69
9. Forgiving Your Siblings 79
10. Forgiving Your Children 95
11. Forgiving Your Spouse or Life Partner 101
12. Forgiving Your Parents 109
13. Forgiving Chronic or Serious Illnesses 133
14. Forgiving Sexual Assault and Child Molestation ... 147
15. Communication Contamination 153
16. Establishing Boundaries 161
17. Releasing Relationships 167
18. Mindfulness Exercises & Meditations 171
19. Obstacle Busters 179
20. Seeking Forgiveness from Others 183
21. Epilogue. Closing Thoughts 189

APPENDIX A: Bibliography 193
APPENDIX B: Poetic Reflections 195

ACKNOWLEDGEMENTS

IN LIFE, NOTHING OF VALUE is ever accomplished alone. Every person and experience, even the arduous ones, has offered me an opportunity for learning, personal growth and determined resilience. Sometimes I wish I didn't have so many challenges and obstacles, but, hey, that's life. Those acknowledged below have influenced my life in deeply meaningful ways.

To Kenny, who patiently listened to my ideas, offered his own insights, and encouraged me every step of the way throughout the writing of this book.

To Lynne Hoffman, for all of your help and support. Thank you for always being there.

To Kimberly Taylor, for your spiritual guidance and insights.

To my mom, in heaven. I think about you every day, I miss you, and I feel your presence with me, especially during the difficult moments.

To my biological mother, who gave me the gift of life, and made a selfless sacrifice. I believe that I will get to meet you in the afterlife.

To my nephew Richie, in heaven, who profoundly touched the lives of so many, including mine, during his brief life. I miss our talks. You will never be forgotten, and your memory will remain in my heart forever.

To my fur babies, Penelope, Alex, and Patrick (in heaven)— who have shown me what it feels like to be loved unconditionally.

To all those who have graciously shared their stories, experiences, insights, and wisdom. Thank you for allowing me to learn through your honest sharing.

Last but not least, to all of the unnamed difficult people who have crossed my life path. You have been my greatest teachers, by offering me the challenge and the opportunity to forgive you.

FORWARD BOUND

I'm turning my back to the wind,
and waving goodbye to the should-have-beens.
Walking away from yesterday,
and breathing the air of a fresh new day.

The days too quickly fly away
when we're too glued to yesterday.
The past has weighed me down too long.
Today I'm choosing a new song.

Walking with my head held high
my eyes are forward bound.
The past is gone. I'm moving on.
It's time to spread my wings and fly!

The sun has set on yesteryear.
I'm done with shedding rusty tears.
I see my life with fresh new eyes.
I've finally bid the past goodbye.

Walking with my head held high
my heart is forward bound.
The past is gone. I'm moving on.
as I spread my wings and fly!"

Nella Coiro

I

INTRODUCTION

"The past has weighed me down too long.
Today I'm choosing a new song."

IF YOU TOLD ME A DECADE AGO, that someday I would write a book about forgiveness, I would have looked at you as if you were completely insane; especially if we were acquainted, and you knew how I felt about this. My world did not have the word *forgiveness* in its vocabulary. And yet… fast forward… here I am writing this book. Life definitely has a sense of humor.

If I reflect back to my teenage years with complete honesty, I recall responding to an apology with the words, "Sorry didn't do it." I did not want to hear an apology, because I was deeply offended. Hidden behind my flippant response, however, were the feelings of a hurt little girl.

Actually, a more honest response would have been, "Why did you hurt me in the first place? I trusted you, allowed myself to be vulnerable, and now I feel hurt." Back then, I was very guarded and super-sensitive, and I was afraid to openly share my feelings. I did not want the person to know that I felt deeply offended, so I pretended that I didn't care. I rationalized my indignation, and chose a defensive stance. I could not let go of my hurt feelings, or find it in my heart to forgive.

Now, it's difficult to believe that I was this person. That was a long time ago. As a result of many life challenges, experiences, struggles, I am a different woman today. For that, I am so glad. I also view life quite differently. After decades of reflection, introspection, and the willingness to work on myself, I have changed. I also think that perhaps the accumulation of years has a way of softening our sharper edges.

Back then, I did not understand that these grudges were weighing me down, and preventing me from living my life to the fullest. Now, I can see that I spent a great deal of time carrying around cumbersome baggage, filled with a lifetime of resentments. I dragged this luggage around with me through every waking moment. No wonder I was so weary and anxious all the time. Who wouldn't be?

I did not realize that I had the ability to let go of this baggage at any given moment. Like Dorothy, in The Wizard of Oz, I have always had the power within me. Yet, nothing truly exists until we are able and ready see it. As I began to change my perception, and I realized that I was carrying the burden of someone else's bad behavior or hurtful words, (and this was only hurting *me*), my life began to transform.

Think about a time when someone has hurt you so deeply, that you felt as if you would never recover. Perhaps you felt as if your heart was ripped out of your chest and set on fire. I have been there a number of times. My heart felt torn, shattered, and shredded to pieces. It took quite a while to fully recover. Eventually, I *did* recover, and you can, too.

Has someone hurt you, and you are finding it difficult to move past this hurt and forgive the offender? I want to begin by telling you that I am so sorry for your pain. You did not deserve it. Some people can be insensitive, thoughtless, or simply clueless. If the person never gave you the apology that you needed and deserved, then please listen to my words: On behalf of that individual, I want to tell you that I'm sorry for the pain and the hurt that this individual caused. If you were standing in front of me, I would give you a big hug.

At different times in our lives, we have all been in the role of the offended party, and, if we are honest with ourselves, chances are that we have also offended others. Let's face it, if we live long enough, people will hurt us, and we are going to hurt others.

We are all imperfect human beings, and sometimes we speak before thinking. Unfortunately, we cannot hit the delete button and eradicate the spoken word. Even when we realize that we are wrong, sometimes it can be difficult to admit this.

When we feel that we have been deeply wounded, it can be devastating. It is so easy to let these wounds define and control us. In doing so, we give away our power. If you want to rid yourself of the debilitating pain of chronic anger and resentment, you *can* learn how to forgive, let go, move forward, and live your best life. Since you have chosen to read this book, you are taking an important first step.

The forgiveness journey can be challenging. Your old wounds will need to be re-examined before they can be healed. Initially, there will be some moments of pain. Gradually, the pain in your heart will dissolve, and it will be replaced with the soothing feeling of serenity. You will experience a major shift within you.

Forgiveness is extremely powerful, and it has a ripple effect. It will gradually, yet profoundly, touch every area of your life. You will experience a deep sense of spiritual and emotional resilience, as you tap into your inner strength. It's an awesome feeling.

THEN AND NOW

Prior to completing my forgiveness work, even the smallest challenge felt insurmountable. I swam against the tide on a daily basis. I did every task the hard way. My entire life was saturated with unnecessary worry and anxiety. The path of greater resistance was often my chosen option. I felt consumed by constant turmoil, and I lived my life similar to that of a soldier on a battlefield.

I was still an angry and scared little girl beneath the armor, and I continued to carry my childhood resentments. I worked diligently at pushing people away (out of fear), and I vehemently embraced my victim stories. I could not let go of this burden, even though it made my life miserable. For these reasons, I simply could not maintain any level of peace for very long.

So… life continued to happen. When situations went wrong, I diverted the blame, or I blamed my current struggles on my unresolved childhood struggles. When I was finally ready to forgive, my life completely transformed. My anger, self-defeating behaviors, and inner turmoil dissolved. I finally achieved the inner peace and serenity that I so desperately wanted.

When I think about the person I used to be, it feels as if I'm watching a movie about someone else. I don't recognize that woman anymore. I am so glad. I can't adequately express how grateful I am that I was given the opportunity, and had the motivation, to change my life. My hope is that you can identify with some of my experiences, and possibly avoid some of the roadblocks that I encountered.

Change and forgiveness involve a process. Unfortunately we can't wave a magic wand and become instantly transformed. Do you hate the word *process*? I know that I did. When something involves a process, this means that we need to have patience, because changes won't happen immediately. I have always lacked patience. I used to cringe when people told drawn-out stories. I wanted to hear the summary and get to the ending quickly.

My work with forgiveness has taught me to be more patient, because I had to proceed through steps and stages. The process takes work, and it requires a great deal of intestinal fortitude. The good news is that when you shed the shackles of resentment, you will be forever changed in unimaginable ways.

Many years ago (when I was struggling with forgiveness), a counselor told me that the best revenge was to live a good life. I looked at her as if she had two heads. My mind and my heart were not ready to process this truth. It took decades to fully comprehend this message—wasted time.

Many of my deepest wounds and resentments dated back to childhood, and, at that time, I felt that they were simply unforgivable. Since I believed that many of my adult struggles were due to the inability to come to terms with childhood experiences, I saw myself as a victim rather than a survivor. In fact, there was a time in my life where I was so consumed with my painful childhood recollections, that I was unable to recall one *good* childhood memory. After I completed my forgiveness work, however, many pleasant memories returned.

When we are in a state of unforgiveness, it can change and shape us to the point where we might not recognize ourselves. Sometimes this change eludes us, and is more apparent to our loved ones. When someone is in a chronic state of anger, it doesn't only affect the angry party; everyone around them is influenced in negative ways. It is impossible to live our lives in a state of resentment without touching the lives of others.

Our memories are capable of making us miserable, especially when we insist upon re-living them over and over again. In doing so, they eventually take on a life of their own. Ideally, we would like to simply erase the upsetting memories, and retain the pleasant ones. Unfortunately, it doesn't work that way. We are not computers.

Since we cannot hit the delete button, we are left with three choices. We can continue holding a grudge, replaying our memories, like a sad song. We can temporarily escape our anger and resentment through our negative behaviors (which will eventually create additional problems), or we can work toward forgiving the offense, letting go, and moving on.

How to Use This Book

Before you continue, please close your eyes, and reach deep into your heart. Without analyzing, bring forth whatever beliefs that you currently have about forgiveness. Now imagine putting these ideas into a box, and closing the lid. Tell yourself that you can open this box again after you finish reading this book.

I have written each chapter to guide you through the various aspects of the forgiveness journey, and offer you the tools and the insights that were helpful to me on my journey. I have also included interviews and beautifully shared insights from others.

My path included a series of trials and errors, but I am

hoping that this book will help you, and give you an opportunity to avoid some of the obstacles that I encountered. Many of the chapters also include insights and wisdom from those whom I have interviewed.

In chapter two, we will explore the various views, and the common misconceptions concerning forgiveness. Chapter three will explore the health benefits, and some fascinating science and research studies. In the fourth chapter, we will look at the Law of Attraction, and how the negative energy of resentments, can attract negative situations and circumstances.

In chapters five and six, we will explore some of the common obstacles which prevent us from moving forward. These include clinging to our victim stories, and escaping through addictive and self-defeating behaviors. Chapter seven will address negative self-talk, self-defeating scripts, and skills to assist you in achieving self-forgiveness. In chapter eight, we will walk, step-by-step, through the forgiveness journey.

In chapters nine, ten, and eleven, we will look at the particulars related to forgiveness and family members. These chapters include reflective and focused insights, as well as specific concerns related to forgiving siblings, children and spouses or life partners. In the twelfth chapter, we will explore the complexities of parental relationships in great detail, and walk, step-by-step, through the process of forgiving our parents.

Chapter thirteen will explore forgiveness and resentment from a different perspective. In this chapter, we are going to look at the challenges of forgiving chronic, progressive, and serious illnesses, including the grief process, coping skills, and the learning opportunities.

Chapter fourteen will look at the struggle inherent in forgiving the serious offenses of sexual assault, and child molestation. Chapter fifteen will look at the communication issues that lead to misunderstandings, including cognitive and memory biases, and body language.

Chapter sixteen will focus upon setting and re-establishing relationship boundaries, while chapter seventeen will explore situations where we must detach from unhealthy relationships.

Chapters eighteen and nineteen will gently guide you through mindfulness exercises, healing meditations, obstacle busters, and healing ceremonies. In chapter twenty, we will explore the various aspects of seeking forgiveness from others.

In conclusion, the epilogue in chapter twenty-one will share some closing thoughts and insights. My hope is that, when you complete your forgiveness journey, you too, will experience, an evolution of the heart.

2

WHAT IS FORGIVENESS?

"Forgiveness is an act of self-compassion."

WHAT IS IT ABOUT THE IDEA OF FORGIVENESS that makes people cringe? So many people see it as surrendering or losing a war. In fact, the mere thought of forgiveness feels like defeat. Perhaps there are just too many misconceptions that contribute to this confusion.

Beyond all of the misunderstanding, what exactly *is* forgiveness?

- Forgiveness is a shift in perception.
- Forgiveness allows us to view the offenses and offenders in a different way.
- Forgiveness heals our hearts.
- Forgiveness allows us to let go of the negative feelings, and to move forward.
- The focus is on us, and not the offender.
- Forgiving is giving up the desire to retaliate.
- The work is done within our hearts, without any contact with the offender.
- Forgiveness is an act of self-preservation, not an act of self-sacrifice.
- Forgiveness may or may not include reconciliation.
- Forgiveness is an act of self-compassion and an opportunity for personal growth.

Forgiveness is a conscious choice that requires preliminary work. This work will bring your heart to a place of readiness, and that is what this book is about. When I completed this journey, my life was transformed in ways that I could never have imagined, and this can happen for you as well.

I have also spoken to many individuals, who have graciously shared their time and their views concerning their own forgiveness journeys. Some of these stories, which particularly touched my heart, are shared throughout this book. I hope that some of these stories will resonate with you as well.

When I asked individuals to share their definitions of forgiveness, I received some very insightful responses. Here are some highlights with accompanying commentary:

Lisa's definition of forgiveness is, *"When I stop keeping count of how many times someone has done something to me."* This definition illustrates that we can obsess about an offense so much, that it prevents us from living our lives. Have you ever kept a mental tally of offenses?

This is Heather's definition: *"When I stopped feeling a knot in my stomach, every time I thought about my ex-husband."* How many of us experience physical discomfort when we think about particular people? Lower back pain? Headaches? Nausea? Sometimes, the mere thought of someone can elevate our blood pressure. Why are we giving this person so much power over our feelings and our bodies?

Mike believes that forgiveness is *"giving up wanting revenge."* This can be a big hurdle to overcome. Often, when we have been hurt, our first thought is retaliation. Since we are suffering, we want the offender to suffer too. Somehow, we think that if the individual experiences the pain that they have inflicted upon us, this will lessen our distress, or even the score. Actually, it doesn't.

In reality, even if the offender encounters misfortune, this will not alleviate our pain. We cannot erase an offense by creating another offense, and revenge will not give us the relief that we might be hoping for. Besides, how can we really justify behaving badly, when this same type of behavior hurt us? As Gandhi said, "An eye for an eye, and soon the whole world is blind."

Jeff shared that forgiveness included, *"letting go of the inner conflicts toward the person."* It is very uncomfortable to have contrasting feelings toward someone. This can occur if we're not sure if we want to remain in the relationship. If we are struggling with this decision, then the relationship must be important to us. Can you forgive the individual and trust again? In Jeff's experience, forgiving helped him to release his conflicts toward the person who hurt him.

Julia saw forgiveness as, *"a gift that we give to someone who might not deserve it."* This is a common belief about forgiveness. We feel that we are giving someone an *undeserved* gift by forgiving them. Let's explore this further. Some people are not remorseful and will never admit that they are wrong. They will attempt to justify their behavior until they take their last breath. Do they deserve to be forgiven? Maybe not. That's not important. When we forgive, we are giving a gift to *ourselves*, not the other person. Keep in mind that you never have to look at or talk to that person again. You just need to let go of the resentment, which is dragging *you* down.

The wrongdoings of others will eventually catch up to them. If you live long enough, you will see that life is a boomerang. Our unkind words and actions return to us. Karma is a loan that yields high interest, and it's simply a matter of time. Just have patience, relax, and let karma do its job. It never disappoints.

Brian shared, *"It took years to forgive my father for beating me when I was a boy. First, I had to stop telling myself that things should have been different."* Many of us wish that we could go back, change the past, and erase those lingering memories that still hurt our hearts. When we are addressing our childhood wounds, the fantasy of rewriting the past is so alluring. Besides forgiveness, we have the added burden of grieving the loss of a normal or a stress-free childhood. In the chapter, *Forgiving your Parents,* this topic is explored in greater detail. For purposes here, and as Brian has asserted, we need to let go of wishful thinking before we can fully forgive.

Kristen shared that *"forgiveness included setting new boundaries with my husband, Max. In the past, I tried to ignore his constant criticisms, I felt hurt and angry. Eventually I developed a grudge.*

When I spoke with him about this, he said that he didn't realize that his comments were hurtful. Max told me that his dad constantly criticized him. Nothing he did was ever good enough. He never told me about this."

Kristen's conversation with her husband invited a dialogue that allowed him to share some of his unhappy childhood experiences. According to Kristen, since their talk, he has became more aware of when his comments seemed critical, and their relationship and their communication has improved significantly.

Although none of us appreciate being judged or criticized, we have all done this at one time or another. Sometimes, we don't realize this unless someone brings it to our attention. Likewise, we should give the other person the benefit of the doubt until we receive information that proves otherwise.

Kristen talked about boundaries. Establishing boundaries can be seen as setting the rules to a game. At the onset, each party clearly understands what is expected of them. There is no guesswork. If Kristen had not shared her feelings with Max, and re-established her boundaries, her husband would have probably continued his behavior. (Refer to chapter sixteen for further discussion on boundaries.)

Forgiveness is the only way to heal our hearts. There aren't any shortcuts or hacks. It is a step-by-step process, and includes erasing the contamination of the past that has tainted our present. When we do this, we are creating a space for a fresh start. It is truly a gift that we give to ourselves.

MISCONCEPTIONS

Now that we have explored some views concerning forgiveness, let's take a look at some of the false impressions. First, forgiveness *does not* require us to communicate directly with the person we wish to forgive. You do not need to approach the individual and say, "I forgive you." Maybe the individual is deceased or is unavailable. Perhaps the person does not want to speak with you. That's okay. Direct verbal communication is not necessary in order to forgive someone.

Second, forgiveness is *not* surrender. We are not conceding defeat when we forgive someone. The opposite is actually true. We are trading in upset and pain, and gaining freedom and relief. We are taking back our power and control of our lives. These feelings are empowering and heart-healing.

Third, forgiveness does *not* mean pretending that everything is okay, and that nothing happened. This is denial, and is a defense mechanism. Pretending that an event never existed can lead to other issues, including addictive behavior. Forgiveness is acknowledging that something indeed happened, and we are willing to forgive the offense and release the debt.

When we try to deny our feelings, they just don't go away. Rather, they influence our physical and emotional health. This can cause us to feel chronically short-tempered, irritable, anxious, or depressed. Physically, this denial can elevate our blood pressure, heart rate, and activate our fight/flight stress response, which releases stress hormones in our bodies. The mind-body connection is fully explored in the next chapter.

Fourth, forgiveness is *not* contingent upon an apology. When we expect an apology, we are placing the power to heal in the other person's hands. We could wait a lifetime and never receive an apology. Some people will not own their poor behavior. Moreover, if the person has passed on, then the opportunity for an apology has also died.

It is also important to note that forgiving is *not* condoning or trying to force ourselves to forget the offense and it's consequences. When we forgive someone, this does not mean that we approve of that person's hurtful behavior. Forgiveness is not about making excuses or accepting the unacceptable. There's an old phrase: "Forgive and forget", and that's easier said than done. In reality, there are some offenses that we will never forget. In these cases, it would be helpful to practice the thought-controlling, mindfulness exercises, and meditations, that are shared in the latter part of this book. They are very effective.

Last, forgiveness *does not* necessarily include reconciliation. Forgiveness happens within your own heart. If you so choose, you never have to speak to your offender again, and that's okay. You will need to carefully weigh the pros and cons of continuing a relationship with the individual. Can the relationship be healthy? Can you trust that person again? Is the relationship toxic or dangerous? Is it healthier for you to keep a distance or completely sever ties? Do you need to set new and clearer boundaries? It is best to re-visit these questions upon completion of the forgiveness process.

Can we reconcile *without* forgiving? Although forgiveness might not include reconciliation, you cannot have a true reconciliation *without* forgiveness. This would simply be a superficial relationship with underlying, unfinished business. A relationship cannot sustain longevity if there is underlying resentment. Eventually, these feelings will re-surface. When there is dormant hostility, even the slightest disagreement can escalate into a feud.

Ultimately, forgiveness is about *personal freedom.* If we believe that we cannot let go of our anger, until the other person changes or apologizes, we are giving them the power to control our feelings and our lives. This thinking keeps us in a self-imposed psychological prison. Forgiveness opens the prison gates.

CLOSING THOUGHTS

When we are shackled with the chains of resentment, our thinking is emotionally-driven and devoid of reason and logic. We might be so comfortable within our self-righteous anger, that we can delude ourselves into believing that our anger is punishing the offender. Actually, the opposite is true. We are continuing to victimize ourselves.

We might attempt to justify our anger by replaying the *if-only's* in our minds. *If only she would apologize. If only he was remorseful.* We delude ourselves into believing our grudge and our anger is being controlled by what that offender will or will not say or do. *If only* that person would do what we wish, then we will give ourselves permission to feel differently. What? Nonsense.

Many years ago, I had a friend who would often say, "You can't get water from a dry well." This has always been a powerful visual. Likewise, we cannot rely upon others to give us what they are incapable of giving (dry wells). We must learn how to give *ourselves* what we need and to nurture our own needs. As we begin to depend upon ourselves, and we reduce our expectations of others, our disappointment will diminish as well.

3
THE SCIENCE OF FORGIVENESS

"Forgiveness enhances our resilience, and assists us in maintaining a healthy balance in our lives."

WHOEVER COINED THE PHRASE, "Your issues are in your tissues," was spot-on! Our emotional baggage immediately finds its way into our physical bodies, creating disruption and un-ease. There have been several studies linking emotional distress to physical illness. I will share some of the most prominent research.

According to the studies conducted at the Mayo Clinic, forgiving and letting go of resentments can improve our physical and emotional health, leading to:

- Healthier relationships
- Improved mental and physical health
- Less anxiety, stress and hostility
- Lower blood pressure
- Less symptoms of depression
- A healthier immune system
- Improved cardiac health
- Increased self-esteem

When we experience a hurtful incident, our body responds by releasing stress hormones, and our heart rate and blood pressure increase. Each time we recollect a hurtful incident, we experience another stress response, as if it is actually occurring again. Our thoughts are very powerful.

Dr. Amit Sood is a Professor at the Mayo Clinic and Chair of the Mayo Mind Body Initiative. He is best known for his work in Stress Management and Resiliency Training, which embraces the disciplines of neuroscience, psychology, spirituality and philosophy. Sood asserts that 40-50% of our happiness depends upon our focus and the choices we make. He claims that we can either focus upon the positive aspects of our lives, or we can choose to ruminate about the negative circumstances surrounding us. This is a conscious effort.

His studies indicate that our thoughts wander between half to two-thirds of the day, many of our thoughts are negative, and we have a strong tendency to focus on the negatives. This tendency dates back to mankind's beginnings and the development of survival skills. Vigilance meant survival.

Since we still retain this inherent survival disposition, our thoughts keep us in a state of continuous stress. To discard negative emotions quickly, we need to practice mindfulness exercises. These exercises include gratitude, compassion, acceptance, life purpose and … yes, you've guessed it... forgiveness.

Gratitude is being thankful for our blessings, and discovering the learning lessons in our negative experiences. This can be difficult when we are dealing with life challenges. It helps to remind ourselves that there are other people who might be hurting more than we are, and reach out to offer our support.

Compassion is about empathizing with others, and offering comfort and words of encouragement. We also need to be kind to ourselves. Sood suggests that we love ourselves like our animal companions love us. Now, that's a whole lot of love!

Acceptance is going along with the flow of life. In other words, *Don't sweat the small stuff*. The older I become, the more I realize that most things are *small stuff*. I can't remember what I worried about five years ago or five days ago. Can you? So, how important was it?

Acceptance does not mean being a doormat or allowing others to mistreat us. It is not submission. It means letting go of what we cannot control, so we can save our energy to address what we *can* control. We need to look at our situations, and say to ourselves, "OK, this has happened. Now what can I do about it?" If we can change the situation, great! If not, we need to let it go and move on.

Life Meaning is about pondering our reason for being here, and discovering our life purpose. I think that most of us want to contribute to making the world a better place. When we work toward this effort, this helps us to find meaning in our lives. All religious and spiritual traditions emphasize the idea of being kind, and helping others. This is reflected in the Golden Rule, which emphasizes treating others with respect and kindness. In Judaism, this is called *Tikkun Olam*, which means to heal or repair the world.

The final mindfulness exercise is *Forgiveness*. Sood believes that our entire world dramatically changes when we forgive, and we see this as a gift that we give to ourselves. His research findings contend that forgiveness strengthens us during times of adversity, enhances our resilience, and assists us in maintaining a healthy balance in our lives.

Since 1985, *Dr. Robert Enright*, Professor of Educational Psychology and Founder of The International Forgiveness Institute, has been conducting Peer-Reviewed Empirical Studies. He has been called *the forgiveness trailblazer*, by Time Magazine, cited as *the father of forgiveness research*, by The Christian Science Monitor, and dubbed *the guru of forgiveness* by the L.A. Times.

Enright's research, done in conjunction with the University of Wisconsin-Madison, and featured in over 100 publications, was very compelling and revealing. Here are some of the highlights:

SEXUAL ABUSE/INCEST SURVIVORS AND
SUBSTANCE-DEPENDENT CLIENTS

After a 14 month period, those in the forgiveness group became emotionally healthier than the control group. Moreover, the craving for drugs decreased in the substance-dependent clients in this group. Differences between the groups were also observed for depression, anxiety, hope and self-esteem. Improvements were observed in the forgiveness group.

Cardiac Patients
After learning forgiveness techniques, individuals in the forgiveness group exhibited better functioning arteries, demonstrated by reduced chest pain. Additionally, their emotional health improved.

Emotionally-Abused Women
Results were similar to the above studies, and included a decrease in anxiety, depression, PTSD symptoms, and an increase in self-esteem.

Terminally-Ill, Elderly Cancer Patients
After four weeks, the forgiveness group showed increased improvement in emotional health. Their anger decreased, and their hopefulness increased.

Women with Fibromyalgia, Who Were Also Child Abuse Survivors
The forgiveness training eased the group's physical symptoms, and helped these women to improve their mental health.

At-Risk Female Adolescents in Korea
This research focused on Korean students who were bullied, and who had bullied others. Those in the forgiveness group demonstrated improvements in emotional health, academic performance, and a decrease in aggressive behavior.

OTHER STUDIES:

Suppressed Anger and Breast Cancer
In 1977, Pettingale, Greer, & Tee studied 160 women over a two-year period, prior to a diagnosis of breast cancer, and then after the diagnosis was made.

The researchers measured the expression of anger, and serum immunoglobulins. This data was measured before their surgery, at three months, at twelve months, and two years after surgery. IgA levels were found to be significantly higher in patients who habitually suppressed their anger. IgA levels are antibodies that are implicated in some autoimmune diseases. The results suggested that how one expresses anger is a contributing factor in the development of breast cancer.

Anger and Cancer Patients

In 2000, Groer, Davis, Droppleman, Mozingo, and Pierce noted that cancer patients displayed "extremely low" anger scores. (There are various reasons for low anger scores, including suppression or restraint.) Other studies also indicated a correlation between the development and progression of cancer, and suppressed anger.

Hendricks, Gore, Aslinia, & Morris (2013) assert that an unhealthy expression of anger can lower one's immune system. When we are angry, our body releases the stress hormone, cortisol. Excessive cortisol in the body can create blood sugar imbalances, suppressed thyroid function, and a decrease in bone density. In turn, these hormonal imbalances eventually compromise the immune system.

Other studies indicate that people who are chronically angry are more susceptible to colds, flus, arthritis, respiratory problems, and asthma attacks, than those who are not chronically angry. Anger is one of the byproducts of ongoing resentment.

THOUGHTS AND FEELINGS CHANGE BRAIN FUNCTION

In his book, *Healing the Hardware of the Soul*, Dr. Daniel Amen asserts that our thoughts, feelings, and behaviors, impact upon our brain function. Through the use of a neuro-imaging technique called the SPECT scan, Dr. Amen studied the connection between blood flow patterns in the brain and behaviors.

He discovered that when an individual is experiencing negative thoughts and emotions, blood flow decreases in the left side of the brain. Since your left temporal lobe is receiving less blood flow, you might experience feelings of fear and anxiety. These negative feelings create anger and frustration as well as negative behaviors.

CLOSING THOUGHTS

As you can see, there have been numerous research studies that address the physical effects of negative feelings such as holding grudges, and the healing aspects of forgiveness. The mind-body connection is powerful. It is interesting to note that the ability to forgive has helped individuals with various medical conditions, including cancer. Anxiety, depression, insomnia, and high blood pressure, are also eased when we are able to exercise forgiveness.

4
THE LAW OF ATTRACTION AND FORGIVENESS

*"As human magnets, every second of our lives,
we send out our thoughts and emotions,
and attract back more of what we have put out."*

ACCORDING TO THE LAW OF ATTRACTION, we are all human magnets. Moreover, we will attract circumstances into our lives based upon our beliefs, thoughts, words, and actions. Our thoughts create a very real and specific vibration or energy frequency, and that energy will seek its vibrational match. Therefore, if we focus on negative thoughts that contain low vibrational energy, we will attract negative situations that share this same energy frequency.

As human magnets, every second of our lives, we send out the energy of our thoughts and emotions, and attract back more of what we have put out. As science continues to study the limitless possibilities of the mind and energy connections, we will learn more about the power we have over our thoughts and our experiences. This new knowledge is intriguing and optimistic, because it proves that we have the power to alter the circumstances of our lives.

Marianne Williamson, author and spiritual teacher, believes that our greatest fear is not that we are inadequate. Rather, we are really terrified by the thought that our power and potential might be boundless. This is an interesting point of view, because it suggests that we are more frightened by success than failure. If you think about it, this makes perfect sense. Success brings bigger challenges, more responsibilities, lifestyle changes, as well as uncertainties.

How does it feel to think that you have the power to create your reality? Is is exciting yet frightening? Take a couple of moments to write down the ways in which your life could change if you truly believed this.

How does this connect with forgiveness? As we begin to recognize the relationship between our thoughts and our experiences, this can help us to become action-focused thinkers, and take control of our negative thoughts. When we cannot forgive, we obsess about the offense. Our thoughts are negative. We feel angry, vindictive, depressed, anxious, and disappointed. These thoughts and feelings, which carry low frequency energy, will attract circumstances with this same energy.

Let's take a closer look at the seven laws of attraction, and connect the dots.

ONE: THE LAW OF MANIFESTATION

This law explains that what we constantly focus upon will manifest in our lives. Everything that we think about is mirrored in our outside world. Since our mind is a powerful manifestation tool, if we increase our positive thoughts, we will attract positive outcomes.

Our conscious thoughts are a choice, and we have the ability to control and change them. We *choose* to focus our awareness in the present moment. We *choose* to prioritize what we think is important. We also *choose* our core values. Therefore, our self-monitoring questions should be: What am I focusing my consciousness upon right now? What can this consciousness create for me?

TWO: THE LAW OF MAGNETISM

The Law of Attraction is always at work. We attract everything into our lives, and this all begins with our thoughts. The energy that we put out will return to us, if it's on the same frequency.

This law is consistent with the laws of karma, which asserts that we reap what we sow; as the ever-familiar phrase asserts, "What goes around comes around."

The universe is filled with vibrations called *strings of energy*. This energy constantly moves within us and around us, even though we are unaware of it. We are all a part of an enormous exchange and expansion of this universal energy. More importantly, we can only attract the energy frequency that we emit.

THREE: THE LAW OF UNWAVERING DESIRE

This law says that if we want to attract positive circumstances into our lives, we need to focus upon achieving our goals, thinking positively, and rid ourselves of doubt. In other words, *act as if*. When we are driven by pure intention, without fear and doubt, we can be fairly confident that the outcome will be positive. Pure intention means that we truly believe that we are worthy of and deserve what we desire.

FOUR: THE LAW OF DELICATE BALANCE

Everything in the universe works in a balanced manner, and the Law of Delicate Balance says that we must maintain balance by enjoying and appreciating what we have now and always. This is simply gratitude.

We can think about and work toward achieving future goals, but we must do so without becoming obsessed, anxiety ridden, or desperate. Again, we need to create a balance where we can work toward future goals, but still feel grateful for what we currently have.

Desperate feelings attract negative energy, which repels positive outcomes. Therefore, it is important to work toward our goals, but it's equally imperative to understand that we can still be happy and content, even if they do not materialize.

FIVE: THE LAW OF HARMONY

Everything in the universe is in perfect harmony, and everything is connected by energy. We are one of billions of energy sources, yet still connected to all energy sources. It's mind-boggling, isn't it? This law teaches us to work in harmony with the universe, so that we can access our full power.

In practical terms, when we create balance in our lives, we clear a path so that energy can flow without restrictions, since this removes the negative energy that impairs our progress. Balance and energy alignment open the floodgates which allow insight, wisdom, and abundance, to flow in our direction. These exist at the higher energy frequencies.

Have you ever heard the phrase *Go with the flow*? It makes life a lot easier than *swimming against the tide*. Life is much simpler when we save our energy, relax, and simply go with the flow. Thus, working with the law of harmony, rather than fighting against it.

SIX: THE LAW OF RIGHT ACTION

Each day there are countless opportunities to attract either positive or negative energies into our lives. Like the Law of Magnetism, the Law of Right Action asserts that we will inevitably reap what we sow. If we treat people badly, negative circumstances will return to us, like a boomerang. It might take some time, but eventually this will happen. The Hindus and the Buddhists refer to this law as karma. Good deeds bring good karma and positive results, and the opposite is also true.

Our energy is self-perpetuating. If we behave with honor, integrity, dignity, kindness and compassion, these will come back to us to the same degree. If we don't, well… guess whose fault that is?

Even when we think that nobody is watching, God, the Higher Power, or the universe is taking notes. If we want others to treat us fairly and with kindness, we should hold ourselves

to the same standards. When interacting with people, we need to ask ourselves these questions:
"Is my behavior acting in the best interest of the other individual?"
"Am I doing the honorable or loving thing?"
"How would I feel if the situation was reversed?"

SEVEN: THE LAW OF UNIVERSAL INFLUENCE

Like the ripple effect, our energies influence everyone around us, whether or not we know these individuals. Since everyone is connected in some way, our beliefs, thoughts, emotions, and actions, are going to have an effect on other people. The more positive we are, the more of a positive influence we will have upon others and our world.

THE HISTORY OF THE LAW OF ATTRACTION

The main principles of the Law of Attraction are evident in the teachings of many civilizations and religious traditions. The Buddha said, *We are shaped by our thoughts; we become what we think. When the mind is pure, joy follows.* This is the core philosophy of the Law of Attraction.

This Law and its tenets have been seen throughout history, and in the work of many famous poets, artists, scientists and great thinkers, such as Shakespeare, Blake, Emerson, Newton and Beethoven.

QUANTUM PHYSICS

In recent years, quantum physicists have made great strides in learning more about the power of our minds and our thoughts, and how these connect with the universe.

Hopefully, future studies will explore the extent to which our thoughts impact upon our lives and the lives of those around us.

LAW OF ATTRACTION STUDIES

THE WASHINGTON, D.C. MEDITATION EXPERIMENT

In the summer of 1993, 4,000 meditators volunteered to meditate on peace and love. This study was conducted to prove that positive thoughts have the power to reduce the amount of crime activity in high crime area in Washington, D.C. A team of scientists and researchers approached the project without bias, and tested for every imaginable variable.

The results were fascinating. During the month of meditation, crime decreased by 25%, and the researchers were convinced that the positive thoughts of a group of people can change the behavior of strangers. Interesting?

THINK YOUNGER: THE FOUNTAIN OF YOUTH

In 1979, research was conducted on men between the ages of 70-80. This study was designed to explore the differences between the men who fondly remembered their youth, versus the men who made attempts to actually relive their youth.

The first group was asked to talk about their younger days and reminisce about good memories. The second group was asked to actually pretend to be younger. This was accomplished by asking them to surround themselves with the activities, the TV shows, and the music that they listened to during their youth.

The group who pretended to be younger actually demonstrated signs of de-aging. Their arthritis diminished, their blood pressure decreased, and their hearing and sight improved. The thoughts and the imagination of these participants actually reversed some of their physical aging issues. Thoughts are far more powerful than we might realize. This study suggests that our thoughts have the power to change and control our bodies.

DR. EMOTO'S WATER EXPERIMENTS

In 2008, Dr. Masaru Emoto conducted the most famous experiment that demonstrated the incredible power of thought. Emoto proved that human consciousness and positive visualization could change the molecular structure of water.

In this experiment, more than 1,900 participants focused positive feelings of gratitude toward water stored in bottles, which were then frozen, and their crystalline formations inspected. After the thoughts of love and peace, or hate and fear, were projected onto them, Emoto photographed the bottles with the frozen water crystals.

The results were as follows: the frozen water in the bottles that received the positive energy from the messages of hope, peace, love, gratitude and joy created beautiful, symmetrical crystals. The frozen water in the bottles, that received the negative thoughts and messages had disjointed and broken crystals. His experiments concluded that our thoughts and intentions can physically alter the world around us.

THE LAWS OF ATTRACTION AND FORGIVENESS

Can we really remain in a state of unforgiveness and still experience any feelings of serenity or happiness?

When we are harboring resentments, we are living in a realm where there is an absence of love. Here are some interesting questions: If we love one person deeply, but we are harboring anger toward another individual, does that have any effect upon the loving energy that we feel toward the first person? Can the negative energy that we feel toward one person cancel out the positive energy that we feel toward another? Does the negative energy have any influence upon the positive energy? More importantly, can we really divide our feelings, and place them in different places in our hearts?

These questions were presented to individuals who had some familiarity with the Law of Attraction. Here are some of the responses.

Ben said that he did not think that negative energy could influence positive energy. He said, *"I love my wife and my sons.*

In fact, I would give my life to save theirs. I hate my boss. He's nasty and obnoxious. I guess you could say that I can keep my emotions in different compartments in my head. But I can say this. If I'm having a bad day at work, sometimes when I come home, I can be irritable with my wife and my boys."

Stephanie said that when she has a grudge, it dominates her thoughts. *"When I'm angry with someone, that's all I can think about until it's resolved. Does it have an effect on my relationships with those I love? I think that it does. Since I can't get my grudges out of my head, I don't give my family the attention that they deserve, because I'm preoccupied."*

It might be easy to justify why we hate or resent someone who has wronged us – at least, according to our perception and interpretation. Yet, the universe and the Laws of Attraction are not particularly interested in our justifications. Removing or withholding love is a very powerful manipulation of energy. How does it feel when love is removed from your life? Take a moment to reflect upon this. Think about a time when you have lost someone you loved. This might be through desertion, rejection, or even death. Can you feel the intensity that this energy encompasses?

Can we really separate our negative feelings from ourselves? Studies have proven that when we have negative feelings toward someone, it harms our health. Moreover, when we harbor negative feelings, our hearts cannot shake off the residual negative energy. This is why our resentments cause *us* to feel horrible. Moreover, aside from feeling badly, according to the Law of Attraction, we will also attract negative circumstances.

CLOSING THOUGHTS

All of the data and research indicate that our thoughts and intentions can influence our environment in significant ways – consequences and circumstances – crime rates – water molecules – the aging process! Amazing, isn't it?

If we choose to live with kindness and forgiveness in our

hearts, and direct this energy toward those around us, that positive energy will spread to all of our circles of influence and our circumstances. Even if we are presented with challenges in life, we will be better able to handle them with grace and strength, because our thoughts are positive.

Many believe that our positive energy can expand to the universal consciousness of every human being, thus creating a global effect. Besides, practicing these tenets will make us better and happier people. No one can feel peaceful and joyful when they are inundated with negative feelings. Eventually we will experience the negative influences created by these thoughts.

As we work through the steps of forgiveness and release our resentments and victim stories, our energy will change and bring about positive changes in our lives. The negative energy will dissipate and the positive energy will shine.

5

ARE YOU ADDICTED TO YOUR VICTIM STORY?

"We can become so accustomed to living with emotional pain that we don't know how to live without it."

DO YOU THINK ABOUT YOUR RESENTMENTS OFTEN? Do you blame the offender for the negative circumstances in your life?

Do you share your victim story to seek sympathy or validation, and become angry if someone tells you that you need to let go of the past?

Do you identify yourself primarily in terms of your victim story?

Do you compare your story to those with similar stories, yet try to convince others that your pain is worse than theirs?

Can you see that your painful story might be controlling your life?

If you can answer *yes* to any of the above questions, then you might be addicted to your victim story.

As illogical as it might seem, sometimes we can become so accustomed to living with emotional pain, that we don't know how to live without it. As soon as one source of pain is resolved, we look for other sources of pain to fill the void. This is because we find comfort in the familiar, even when the familiar feels horrible. We are comfortable with being uncomfortable. We know what to expect, and there are no surprises.

Our victim story can gradually consume our entire identity, as we become more comfortable in this role and some of its perks. (Getting attention and sympathy.) Therefore, when we let go of our resentments, we will need to find a way to fill the void, and redefine ourselves without these roles. This unknown territory can evoke new levels of anxiety.

Moreover, clinging to our victim stories can provide us with a valid excuse for anything that goes wrong in our lives. "If this didn't happen to me, then x, y and z would not have happened." Over time, it can become convenient to maintain this position, because it frees us from taking ownership for our lives, as we continue to divert the blame elsewhere.

FROM VICTIMIZATION TO VICTIMHOOD

If you do not forgive the people who have wronged you, eventually, you will move from a state of victimization to a state of victimhood. There is a huge difference. Victimization describes an event that happened to you, while victimhood is about your identity. When you get stuck in the victim stage for a long period of time, it begins to dominate your life and it defines you. As this happens, you have progressed into the state of victimhood. Before you realize it, you are caught up in a downward spiral, as you see yourself as a victim, and nothing more.

Victimization is the result of a particular offense, while victimhood becomes a lifestyle. If you live in a state of victimhood, you will relate to everything, everyone, and every experience in your world as a victim. You will perceive everything that happens to you as victimization, and you will automatically place the blame on others for every failure or mistake in your life. Every conversation will focus upon your tale of woe. Thus, you have reached a point where you *have become* your story.

There comes a point in our lives where we need to stop blaming others and take responsibility for our choices. This is the pivotal point where we take back our power. As long as we believe that we are victims, we will continue to feel helpless and powerless over our lives. Ruminating over a past offense will eventually cause us to become addicted to our victim stories.

THE PATH OF OUR VICTIM STORY

Since every addiction has an initial payoff, (before it begins destroys your life), a *victim story addiction* will follow this same path. It begins when someone we trust has offended us, and we become overwhelmed with emotions. We feel hurt and angry, and we are not sure how to handle the situation. Rather than letting it go or confronting the individual, we allow these angry and hurtful feelings to fester. Then we give them power by obsessing about them. Voila! Now we have a full-fledged resentment.

CLOSING THOUGHTS

If we chronically ruminate about the our resentments, self-pity and anger increases, our health is negatively influenced, and we begin to approach *all* of our experiences as victims. Eventually, our chronic lamenting will become annoying to those around us, who don't want to hear our story yet again, and will want to run and hide when they see us approaching. After a while, people run out of tolerance and empathy.

If you are addicted to your victim story, you will probably be resistant to hearing advice or possible solutions. All suggestions will be considered unacceptable or unworkable. Why? If you have grown accustomed to talking about your victim stories, what would you talk about when this issue is resolved? When you release your resentments, you will need to develop new conversations. This can be frightening.

Even if you are justified in feeling offended, the lingering resentment will eventually hurt you, and negatively influence your relationships with others. Ask yourself, "Is my victim story making me happy?" If, after careful reflection, your answer is "no", then congratulations! You have just taken a monumental step toward reclaiming your life.

6

PAIN KILLERS OR EMPTINESS FILLERS

*"All addictive behavior begins with the notion
that we can use something outside of us to fix
or erase the uncomfortable feelings within us…
then, we choose our substance or our behavior."*

As your chronic resentments take control of your life, and your emotional pain becomes agonizing, you will want instant relief. At this point, you will search for anything outside of yourself to ease the hurt within. *Pain killers* and *emptiness fillers* will temporarily lift your mood, numb your pain, and soothe your anger. Nevertheless, these short-term solutions create long-term problems, and are ultimately ineffective in resolving your issues.

In this chapter, we will explore the most common external remedies that we use to escape our feelings and hurt. Pain killers and emptiness fillers (as defined here) include substances and other addictive behaviors. Some commonly abused substances are food, sugar, alcohol, or drugs. Behavioral addictions include obsessive-compulsive behaviors, which include shopping, gambling, codependency, unresolved childhood issues, or victimhood addiction (being addicted to victim stories and resentments).

After a while, unresolved resentments will inevitably damage every area of your life. The ongoing, nagging thoughts will begin to imprison you. As you stop living your best life, and your joyfulness ebbs, you might also begin to develop physical illnesses. Often, instead of addressing these issues, many resort to quick-fix, short-term solutions as defined above. All addictive behavior begins with the notion that we can use something outside of us to fix or erase the uncomfortable feelings within us…then, we choose our substance or our behavior.

There are many ways that individuals choose to numb and escape from their feelings. Alcohol has always been a popular choice. It is affordable, legal, and it is as close and accessible as the nearest liquor store, supermarket, pizzeria, diner, or restaurant. Food has always been another great escape. Comfort foods like chocolate and cheese will raise your endorphin levels and give you a brief feeling of euphoria, and sugar will give you a dopamine energy burst, even though sugar crashes can be very unpleasant.

FOOD

I have had food issues in the past, and I can recall feeling the emotional pain melting away, as I temporarily escaped by eating comfort foods. This is called emotional eating. The problem, however, is that the comfort rapidly morphs into discomfort. The euphoria is short-lived when you get on the scale (if you dare), and see that you have gained weight. Yikes! When you fully realize the consequences of your escape-eating, you can crash like a plane on fire, descending from the clouds in a split second. Not fun. At the same time, this surge of reality can be an important turning point, and the opportunity for change.

ALCOHOL

Alcohol is another ineffective pain killer and emptiness filler. In fact, it will probably increase your depression. Alcoholic drinking comes with headaches and hangovers, fatigue and vomiting, and lots of regret. Ask any alcoholic – alcoholism is an equal opportunity destroyer. Ultimately, it solves nothing, but it does delight in creating a slew of other problems.

And yet, alcohol is legal, and, in nearly all cultures, alcohol is socially acceptable. It is encouraged and readily available at all social functions. Can you imagine attending a wedding or any other party without alcoholic beverages? It would be considered rude – unheard of! Alcohol is a *must* at all social gatherings, including barbecues, and especially sports-related parties.

Where is the first place people head toward when they walk into the party room? Yep, you've guessed it – the bar! Alcohol and celebrations walk hand-in-hand. It has become a social norm. This concept is so socially ingrained, that we don't even think about the observations cited above. Even with small gatherings in one's home, the host will ask, *"What would you like to drink?"* Nine times out of ten, the word *drink* means an alcoholic beverage. Interesting, isn't it?

If someone has a pre-disposition toward alcoholism, cultural norms greatly enable this process. In fact, there are social pressures imposed upon those who choose not to drink alcohol. Those who particularly enjoy drinking often ask non-drinkers, the question "Why aren't you drinking?" or, coax them, saying, "Come on. Have a drink. It's a holiday (or party)." This presents challenges to those who prefer not to drink as well as those in recovery, who want to socialize and remain sober.

All of the advertising focuses upon the pleasures of drinking: a romantic evening, a celebration, champagne toasts, and a fun-filled party atmosphere. What they don't highlight are the damaged relationships, drunken outbursts, domestic incidents, car accidents, emergency-room visits, lost jobs, frightened children, health issues, DT's, detoxes, rehabs, and all of other horrors associated with alcohol abuse and addiction. They will say "Drink responsibly" in alcohol advertisements. Yet, they fail to recognize that this is impossible for those who are predisposed toward alcoholism and addiction.

And so, like food, alcohol can easily become a way to escape negative feelings, including anger and resentments.

DRUGS

Drug addiction has become a global epidemic. Legalizing gateway drugs (marijuana) will only make the situation much worse. We are not going to solve a problem by increasing availability. I just don't understand this logic. Easier access, the lack of fear, and a culture that calls drug use "recreational", all contribute to drug abuse, drug addiction, and a very dangerous pain killer and emptiness filler.

Heroin used to be frowned upon, and associated with needles, the poor, and the homeless. Therefore, this problem was not given the attention that it deserved. Now, it has become a huge epidemic, especially among the middle-class and college students. More people are trying it, because it has become available in forms that do not require injections. Therefore, heroin is becoming a major epidemic among the affluent. Now people are taking notice and seeking ways to stop the bleeding.

Unfortunately, due to social media and the internet, drugs are more accessible today than ever before. In my research, I was shocked to discover that there were websites specifically designed for people who experiment with, or who are addicted to illegal drugs. Set up as forums, anonymous individuals ask questions about how to combine various drugs for the "best high,"and tips on how to avoid overdoses. (No, I'm not joking.)

In these forums, people rely upon the advice of complete strangers to make their choices and drug selections. Dangerous? Apparently, these individuals don't think so. And this type of venue contributes to a perfect storm, and easier access to the path of addiction. Chemical changes in the brain, leading to cravings, obsessive-compulsive behavior, bad judgment, poor choices, personality changes, and a journey through hell which ultimately leads to death.

The addiction journey can begin innocently. A party – a few drinks – someone gives you a pill or offers you some cocaine, and you try it. You're curious, or you feel pressured. Maybe you're harboring some uncomfortable feelings and you just want to escape for a while. One person might try it once, and never do it again. Another person is captivated by the feeling, and they want more.

EVAN'S STORY

Evan, who describes himself as a *"quiet guy, on the shy side"*, said that he was hooked from the first time he tried cocaine.

"*I never smoked weed – not my thing, but I'm definitely a guy who loves his beer. I was at a party and one of the guys offered me coke. I admit, I was skeptical at first. Afraid. But my girlfriend just broke up with me, and I was feeling lousy. So, I thought to myself, 'Why not?' One time won't hurt."*

"The problem is the way it made me feel. Not at all like the buzz you get from a few beers. Completely different. I really didn't like the idea of inhaling it at first. But it hits you so fast. It's a weird feeling. All of a sudden, you feel upbeat. Happy. Excited. Everyone and everything around you seems amplified – enhanced. Suddenly, I didn't care that my girlfriend left me. The heartache disappeared."

"I've always had some problems with feeling depressed. As I said, I'm a shy guy, and I get nervous when I'm around a lot of people. I was bullied as a kid, and I think I keep a lot of feelings inside. I'm afraid to get angry at people. Not very good at standing up for myself. After snorting, I felt more confident. Braver. I didn't care what people thought of me. My whole personality seemed to change. It was love at first sight, and I became addicted right away."

"I don't want to go into all of the details. Coke isn't cheap. I learned how to be a good liar, and my dad kept giving me money. In between getting high, my depression got worse. The craving has a life of its own. At the beginning, I loved being this new me. After a while, coke made me into a guy that I began to hate."

"I tried N.A.(Narcotics Anonymous) a couple of times, stood clean for a few weeks, then I relapsed. The last time I used, February 23rd, 2013, I looked in the mirror, and didn't recognize the guy looking back at me. Suddenly, I felt such remorse. I said, 'God, please help me.' I usually only share this part at meetings, but since you said that you

won't use my real name, here goes. I began to cry. I remembered that I had the phone number of my last sponsor in my wallet. I called him up, and he came to my apartment."

"The first thing he asked me was, 'Are you sick and tired of being sick and tired?' With tears in my eyes, I said. 'Yes'. And Barry (my sponsor) said, 'Good. You're ready.' We went out to get something to eat, and then we went to a meeting. A day at a time, I've been clean ever since. I go to meetings every day. My life got better. I have a job. I'm happy. I have learned that drugs – artificial courage – aren't the answer. I've made some great friends. I'm comfortable with myself. Oh, and Barry is still my sponsor."

The resilience of the human spirit has the potential to be boundless. It's one thing to talk about statistics. Numbers are cold, vague and impersonal. It is very different to hear a person's struggle and triumph.

As mentioned earlier, internet access has greatly contributed to a surge in drug abuse and drug-related deaths. There appears to be a level of desensitization today that did not exist in the past. More people are willing to experiment than ever before. Others are trying to compete with one another. Some individuals have resorted to self-destructive antics, simply to get an audience of followers online. Moreover, through social media and other internet sites, people are more easily able to find and connect with those who sell illegal drugs.

According to World Health Organization (WHO), worldwide an estimated 2 billion people abuse alcohol, roughly 185 million people are abusing drugs, and about 1.3 billion are smokers. In 2000, WHO estimates that nearly 12.4% of deaths across the globe were a direct result of alcohol, tobacco, and drug abuse. According to the National Institute of Drug Abuse, overdose deaths involving opioids rose from 8,048 in 1999 to 47,600 in 2017. Opioids include prescription opioids (including methadone), heroin, and other synthetic narcotics (mainly fentanyl).

The Center for Disease Control and Prevention estimates that 88,000 people die annually from alcohol-related causes. 70,237 drug overdose deaths occurred in the United States in 2017.

Opioids—mostly synthetic opioids (other than methadone)—are the main cause of drug overdose deaths. Opioids were involved in 47,600 overdose deaths in 2017 (This was 67.8% of all drug overdose deaths).

NIKKI'S STORY

Have you ever heard someone say, *"I'd rather die than forgive that person?"* According to Nikki, this was her favorite go-to chant, and she nearly drank herself to death. She simply could not forgive her ex-husband, who left her after a five-year marriage. Nikki wanted children and Jake did not. They didn't discuss this before getting married, because Nikki assumed that eventually they would think about starting a family. Her ex-husband never gave any indication that he never wanted children.

She told me, *"I was shocked when I mentioned the possibility of having children, and he became angry and said that he didn't want the added pressure of having kids."* Their relationship spiraled downward, and they argued constantly. Nikki recalled, *"I saw a side of Mark that was so foreign to me. We grew to hate each other, and our relationship deteriorated. Finally, he left me and filed for a divorce."*

For five years following their divorce, Nikki continued to use alcohol as her pain killer. She referred to herself as a *"functional alcoholic,"* because *"my drinking didn't interfere with my job, I would binge drink on weekends… I would think about Mark, get angry, and drown myself in alcohol. Bit by bit, my life began to unravel… When I went to A.A., my sponsor said that I was drinking at him. In other words, I drank out of anger."*

"My sponsor said I needed to forgive him, or I would eventually relapse. So I fired her and got another sponsor, and the she told me the same thing. I was so annoyed. When I protested, she said, 'Nikki, you keep saying you'd rather die than forgive him. So, don't forgive him, go back to drinking, and you'll get your wish.' I needed to think about that."

"I realized that I was a dry drunk. I still had the attitude and the anger, minus the drink. I wasn't really sober. I was abstinent, but still *miserable. Like it or not, ultimately , I had to forgive him. The point is that even if you stop self-medicating, you have to let go of resentments, or you're going to relapse. It might take some time, but it will happen."*

ADDICTIVE AND IMPULSE-CONTROL BEHAVIORS

COMPULSIVE GAMBLING
Compulsive Gambling is a topic that has personal significance to me. It might appear harmless, but it can easily lead to serious debt, financial stress, and relationship issues. Moreover, if the gambler borrows money from loan sharks to support their compulsion, and is unable to repay the debt, they face dire consequences. In the Chapter, *Forgiving Your Parents*, I discuss my father's gambling problem in further detail.

COMPULSIVE BUYING
Addictive shopping is called a Compulsive Buying Disorder (CBD). Most of us are excited when we purchase something new, especially if it is something that we have saved for. Compulsive buyers purchase items because it gives them a euphoric feeling, or a temporary *high*. Their focus is on this feeling rather than on the item purchased.

A Compulsive Buying Disorder includes not only those who overspend, but also those who devote an unusual amount of time browsing or obsessing about purchasing goods. Sometimes these individuals will purchase items and then return them. Like gambling, the inability to control buying impulses can lead to financial difficulties.

CODEPENDENCY
Codependency is often misunderstood. In addiction psychology, the codependent is the partner or family member of someone who has a substance abuse issue. This person is usually an enabler. From a broader perspective, codependency is when

an individual is so dependent upon another person, that they cannot separate who they are from the other individual. Since a codependent lacks all personal boundaries, this individual feels exactly what the other person is feeling. Moreover, the codependent's self-worth and identity are dependent upon the approval of the other individual.

The codependent focuses entirely upon the other individual, and becomes consumed with meeting the other person's needs. As this progresses, the codependent begins to lose autonomy and independence. Anyone can become codependent, but those from dysfunctional or addictive families are more vulnerable than others.

Is codependent behavior a means of emotional escape? Absolutely! Codependency is both a pain killer and an emptiness filler. If we obsessively focus upon someone else, then we are not thinking about our own unresolved issues, are we? What better way to escape our feelings?

Childhood Issues

Unresolved childhood issues are included in this chapter because childhood resentments can be the most difficult to forgive. (See Chapter 12, Forgiving Your Parents.) At the same time, these resentments can be a way to avoid other issues that need to be addressed. In this sense, they are a pain killer.

When we cling to our victim stories, this is a pain killer in the sense that it prevents us from addressing and resolving our grudges. (Victimhood addiction is explored fully in Chapter 5: Are You Addicted to Your Victim Story?)

Trauma Drama

Trauma Drama is another pain killer and an emptiness filler that is often overlooked. Nevertheless, it contains all the components of an addiction. Trauma Drama is the need to create unnecessary drama to feel euphoric. Even the smallest situations are blown out of proportion and seen as major traumas. Everything is a big deal. These individuals are masters at upsetting people and creating disruption. All of this is an unconscious effort to divert the focus away from the real issues. If you grew up in a dysfunctional or a chemically dependent family, then you might recognize the Trauma Drama scenario.

Most of us have met a drama queen. This person embellishes a story, creates fictional scenarios, gossips, and loves to create disturbances?. Then they sit back and enjoy the show. Like a puppet master, they revel in pulling everyone's strings.

Drama queens experience a feeling of euphoria and excitement, because their bodies are reacting to the fight-or-flight response that activate particular chemicals in their bodies. They find that they can replicate this feeling by creating drama, and they become compulsive in their need to do so. Thus, this compulsion shares many of the components of addictive behavior.

CLOSING THOUGHTS

Unresolved resentments create anger, depression, hopelessness, and unhappiness. Moreover, nothing short of forgiveness will provide a permanent solution. Despite this, many resort to addictive behaviors to ease their discomfort.

If you attend any type of twelve-step meeting, you will eventually hear about the dangers of resentments. Resentments are the greatest cause of relapse amongst substance abusers, and a major obstacle that prevents long term *emotional* sobriety for everyone, regardless of their particular issue(s).

When individuals deal with their unresolved resentments by grasping at anything and everything that might provide temporary relief, this eventually leads them down a dark, unhappy, and self-destructive path. As the euphoria dissipates, the resentment and the pain resurface.

Whenever you depend upon something outside of yourself to comfort you and help you to escape, it just doesn't work long-term. Your *emptiness fillers* and *pain killers* might provide temporary relief, but they eventually lead to horrible scenarios.

You can't put a small bandaid on a knife wound and expect it to heal. Resentments are like knife wounds, and the only treatment to heal them is forgiveness.

In order to break bad habits we must replace them with healthier alternatives. Otherwise, we will resort back to old familiar patterns to fill the void. The first step is to acknowledge that we are using self-destructive behavior to escape our pain. Then, take an action. This might include attending a 12-step group, meditation, mindfulness exercises, thought-busting, and obstacle busting techniques. (Refer to chapters 7, 12, 18, and 19 for in-depth explorations.)

The most important step, however, is to transcend your resentments by working through the forgiveness process. This will help you permanently release the grudges that contributed to your addictive behavior in the first place.

7

SELF-FORGIVENESS AND TAMING YOUR INNER CRITIC

*"We need to love ourselves
like our animals love us.
Now, that's a whole lot of love!"*

THE SNEAKY GREMLIN

WE ALL HAVE AN INNER VOICE that denigrates us, berates us, casts doubt upon all of our decisions, and tells us that we are doomed to fail. Left unchecked, this internal critic can terrorize us into a state of frozen fear. Whether we realize it or not, this voice is extremely powerful and oppressive.

It stops us from taking risks and achieving our dreams, steals our serenity, and causes us to feel inferior. In fact, our inner critic is the biggest obstacle preventing us from *forgiving ourselves*. It can convince us that we did something unforgivable, and it can shame us into believing that we are terrible people.

Although we might find it difficult forgive others, it can be far more challenging to forgive ourselves, because this annoying inner voice continually taps on our shoulder and reminds us of our indiscretions. This critic assists us in self-assault, and we can easily become overwhelmed with *should haves*.

The first step in taming our critic is to recognize it. We cannot change what we do not acknowledge. Since our thoughts zoom by with incredible speed, we are not aware of every single thought that we have. This is why we need to make a conscious effort to monitor them. As you begin to monitor your thoughts, you might be very surprised at what you detect.

Negative emotions like shame, doubt, guilt, anxiety, and depression are always the result of critical thoughts. Have you ever had a good day, but then suddenly your mood seemed to shift for no apparent reason? You feel perplexed, and think to yourself: "What happened? I was okay a minute ago." Your mood changed because your inner voice has just criticized you. As you continue to monitor your thoughts, you will become more skilled at making this connection.

TAKING BACK YOUR POWER

The best way to stop this rampant, nagging voice, is to keep a journal. Each time you recognize a self-critical thought, jot it down. This will help you become more aware of exactly what your inner critic is telling you. You will eventually see patterns in your journal.

NEGATIVE SELF-TALK SCRIPTS

These are some of the common negative scripts that we tell ourselves, and they have the ability to influence our moods, motivation, and our entire outlook. They can ignite our fears and insecurities, influence our choices, and stop us from living our best life.

- I shouldn't have done this, or I should have done that.
- I never do anything right…
- I will never succeed…
- I'm cursed. I'm doomed to fail…
- I can't…
- I'll never be…
- I don't deserve…
- Life isn't fair… The odds are against me.

- I'm too old…
- I'm not good enough or attractive enough.
- I have nothing to offer… I'll only be rejected.
- I'm too afraid to…
- They're laughing at me.
- Why me? I don't deserve this.

It's an exhausting list, isn't it?!

As children, we are born with a blank slate, until we are taught, influenced, criticized, and indoctrinated by environmental influences. Parents, families, teachers, authority figures, cultural norms, television, music, traditions, and religion, are all extremely persuasive, and they powerfully influence our inner critics. Beginning at a very young age, we begin to learn *appropriate* behavior specific to gender, cultural roots, age, social class. We also inherit the religious beliefs of our parents, and each religion has its own set of rules. In addition to TV and music, the internet, social media and video games are also extremely influential. These all contribute to our critical thoughts.

WHAT DO YOU THINK?

The average person has between 50,000 to 80,000 thoughts a day and 70% of them are negative. Ninety-five percent of those thoughts are the same as the previous day, and most of them are about the past. Our brains do not stop until we go to sleep. Our thoughts continue throughout our day as we brush our teeth, shower, get dressed, eat, travel, work, socialize, and watch TV.

Most accidents occur because people are daydreaming – usually ruminating over something that happened and cannot be changed. Very often, we are not consciously aware of our ongoing thoughts until we are trying to focus on something, trying to relax, or attempting to fall asleep. If you have ever suffered from insomnia, you might recall that it was difficult to fall asleep because of the unimportant thoughts that were dancing in your mind. The mind can be like a hummingbird that tirelessly flaps its wings with incredible speed.

THOUGHT BUSTERS

It's time to take back your power through self-confrontation and neutralization exercises that I call *Thought Busters*. When you hear your inner critic speaking to you, these techniques are very effective. Try these words: *"Stop! Delete thought. Move on."* This will interrupt your thought pattern and re-direct your thinking. It also allows you to be consciously aware of your current thoughts, and take charge. I have been using these exercises for years, and they are quite effective.

THE S WORD

Guilt occurs when we feel badly about something we have said or done. It is specific to a particular event. *Shame,* however, is an overall feeling of negativity about who we are as a person. It is all-encompassing.

Shame can be debilitating. It can cause us to feed badly about ourselves and contribute to the following problems:

- Self-criticism and self-blame
- Low self-esteem
- Self-neglect and self-destructive behavior
- The belief that you do not deserve anything good in your life.
- Extreme anger
- Rude behavior

Self-forgiveness is the most powerful step you can take to rid yourself of crippling shame, so let's get started. Think about one situation where you know that your behavior was wrong or inappropriate, and it still bothers you. You might have upsetting memories that cause you to feel guilt and shame.

In a few sentences, write down the event and the possible repercussions that it caused. If this situation still influences your life in some way, then it doesn't matter if it happened a long time ago.

Now that you have selected an offense, think about what caused you behave that way, and write down the answers to these questions:
- What was going on in your life at that time?
- Can you recall your thoughts that preceded the event?
- What was happening around you?
- Were you reacting to a previous event that triggered this situation?
- Can you identify anything that might have had an effect on your behavior?
- Did the offense create consequences?
- Are there still ongoing ramifications? What are they?

This information can help you to identify possible triggers that can easily lead you to behave in ways that are against your core values. They can also be very helpful in preventing future conflicts.

SELF-EVALUATION CHECKLIST

Most of the time, it can be easy to identify our weaknesses, but we struggle with recognizing our positive qualities. Frequently, we are far more critical of ourselves than we are of others.

The focus questions below will be helpful in writing your list.
- What do you like about yourself?
- What are your strengths?
- What are your weaknesses?
- What have you learned from your weaknesses?

Ask friends or family members to share one quality about you that they like.

Along with *thought busting*, this exercise will help you to see who you are as a whole person – strengths and flaws.

LEARNING OPPORTUNITIES

Ok, you have made mistakes. We all have. You might have treated someone poorly. Perhaps it was a horrendous lapse in judgement. You will need to take ownership and be willing to make an amend and possible restitution. This amend can be direct or indirect, depending upon the circumstances. In Chapter 20, we will explore this in further detail.

Every mistake is accompanied by a learning opportunity. I have always learned more from my mistakes than from my accomplishments. In fact, many of my achievements were the result of the wisdom incurred through life lessons.

We learn from our inappropriate words or actions. Have you ever opened your mouth before you mind has a chance to censor your words? Then you think to yourself, "Oops", or similar, stronger words? You wish you could go back in time and change the consequences. But you can't. So, instead, you ruminate about the event and beat yourself up. You are caught up in guilt and shame.

We also learn from the things we wanted to do or say, but could not to do so at that moment in time. Many believe that we are haunted the most by those situations where we refrained. We can berate ourselves because of this, or we can learn from it.

Pen and paper at hand, jot down what you have learned from each mistake you have made. Keep in mind that we can learn far more from one faux pas (mishap) than from several successes. When we behave poorly, there are usually consequences. This fallout is a part of the learning lesson.

Although it can be difficult to look in the mirror, sometimes it's worth the effort, especially when we need to forgive ourselves and move forward in our lives. Very often, when faced with the painful memories associated with our indiscretions, we want to hide or divert our attention. This keeps us stuck.

When we continue to push down feelings of shame and disappointment, this energy doesn't dissipate. It is re-directed and translated into physical issues and emotional upset. It simply changes form. All of the exercises explored in this chapter will help you to release your past shame, forgive yourself, and moving forward in your life.

CLOSING THOUGHTS

I strongly believe that we did the best we could with the knowledge and resources available to us at the time. Think back to a mistake you made in an earlier part of your life. It could be a behavior, or angry words that you could not rescind. If you could go back in time and change it, would you? Most of us would chant an emphatic "Yes!"

Life intervenes; it forces us to learn from experiences, grow and change. Behavior that we thought was perfectly acceptable at twenty, sounds immature and just plain dumb when we are forty. That's just a part of our learning journey. *We experience life moving forward, but we only learn through hindsight.*

As you learn to tame and take charge of this critic, you might be amazed at how differently you will begin to feel. Our self-talk has a profound effect upon our emotions and our physical maladies. This is why awareness is an important step in helping us to take charge of the messages that we are giving ourselves.

If you are struggling to forgive yourself for the harm that you might have caused someone else, please refer to Chapter 20: *Seeking Forgiveness from Others*. This chapter will guide you through the process of making an apology, amends and restitution. Remember that you have a right to forgive yourself for being an imperfect person. Beating yourself up is no longer an option.

8

THE FORGIVENESS STEPS

*"The past has weighed me down too long.
Today I'm choosing a new song."*

THE LONGEST VOYAGE TAKES PLACE FROM OUR MINDS to our hearts. On a cognitive level, we all know that it's unhealthy to harbor resentments. This alone, however, will help us to transcend our hurt. How many times have you said to yourself, "I know that this grudge is only hurting me, but I just can't find it in my heart to forgive?" When we feel hurt and offended, our emotions take charge, and our logic steps aside. In order to let go of our resentments, we need to work through these emotions.

The steps in this chapter will help you to work through your feelings, forgive offenses, and release your resentments. With more serious offenses, you might need to progress slowly, or repeat the steps. That's okay, because each time you repeat the process, you will be doing so with an increased level of awareness. As you proceed through these steps, please be aware of any feelings of gradual relief, as your heart releases your resentments, forgives, and begins to heal.

In forgiving our parents, we are presented with a unique challenge as well as an opportunity. Our relationships with our parents are multifaceted and often, complicated. We have particular expectations of our parents that far exceed our expectations of others. Therefore, parental forgiveness work is more intricate, since it involves forgiving a relationship rather than a single, isolated incident. That is why there is a separate chapter and steps for this particular and important forgiveness work. (See Chapter 12: Forgiving Your Parents.)

Forgiving chronic or serious medical illnesses requires specific and additional work. This includes cultivating coping skills and grieving the losses incurred as a result of particular illnesses. Therefore, this process is also explored fully in a separate chapter. This chapter also includes my personal experiences and the experiences of other inspiring and strong women. (See Chapter 13: Forgiving Chronic or Serious Illnesses.)

Before you begin, please make a commitment to yourself that you will approach this process with honesty, open-mindedness, and willingness. Remind yourself that forgiveness is for *you*, and not for the offender. Take a deep breath, and visualize inhaling courage. As you exhale, picture releasing any feelings of anxiety or fear. Now, let's get started.

STEP 1: PREPARATION

Write these words on a piece of paper: "We are all imperfect people, and we make mistakes." Throughout the writing part of your forgiveness work, keep these words in plain view. As you encounter moments where you feel angry or upset, please refer back to these words. This will help to redirect your thinking and perspective, and alleviate your anxiety. It will also assist you in overcoming resistance. It works quite well.

Tools: This exercise should be handwritten, so you will need looseleaf paper or a notebook. There is a power to writing your thoughts with pen and paper, rather than typing or dictating them. Since the action is more personal, you will feel more emotionally attached to the feelings that you are expressing. The process of writing down your thoughts will be extremely helpful in your forgiveness work.

STEP 2: THE LIST

Make a list of anyone who has hurt you in some way, and

whom you have not forgiven. Next to their name, write down the offense. Even if you feel that the offense was trivial, if you still have a grudge, then write it down.

As you look at this list, reflect upon what effect each offense has had upon your life? We are influenced by every experience that we encounter, especially the negative ones. If we feel that we have been offended and we are struggling to forgive, then we have been deeply hurt. We need to acknowledge this.

STEP 3: RATE THE HURT

Next to each name, rate the degree of hurt and pain caused by this individual. Use a scale of one to ten, where number one would indicate the least amount of pain, while the number ten would indicate that the offense and it's consequences were devastating.

In some situations, you might have experienced ongoing difficulties with a particular person. This often happens with family members or employers, where it can be difficult to completely sever ties. If you have an accumulation of resentments, choose a number to summarize the overall level of pain that you have experienced.

STEP 4: REFLECTIVE QUESTIONS

Answer these questions:
- What was your relationship like prior to this event?
- What did each person say or do?
- How did it make you feel? (Try to be specific in identifying your feelings.)
- How has this person's wrongdoing negatively influenced your life?
- Has the offense created an ongoing effect?
- How has it impacted upon your relationship with yourself?
- In what ways has it affected your relationship(s) with others?

- What is your relationship with that person like now?
- Do you feel that you must receive an apology before you can forgive?

Here are some examples:

MIKE'S STORY

Mike's father abandoned him and his mom when he was ten years old. He never saw his dad again, and he doesn't know if the man is still alive. Mike never got over this hurt, and he still has a resentment. In fact, he emphatically asserted, *"I absolutely refuse to forgive him."* His anger has not waned with the passing of time. Because of this emotional scar, Mike has always struggled with intimate relationships, and has strong fears of being abandoned. He described himself as a *"lonely bachelor."*

Rate: 10

- **What did the offender say or do?** *"My dad abandoned me and my mom, when I was a boy."*
- **How did it make you feel?** *"I never got over this hurt, and I just can't forgive him."*
- **How has this offense negatively influenced your life and influenced your relationships with yourself and others?** *"I have always struggled with close relationships, and I usually tend to avoid people. I'm a loner who hates being alone."*
- **What is your relationship with this person like now?** *"I don't know where he is or if he's still alive."*
- **Are you waiting for an apology before you can forgive him?** *"No. It won't change things."*

VERONICA'S STORY

Although four years have passed, Veronica is still angry with her ex-fiancé, George. He was unfaithful, broke the engagement, and then he posted photos of his new girlfriend on social media sites. (That were accessible to her.) Veronica was humiliated, and felt that his actions were cruel. She said, *"How could someone who once loved me, be so hateful?"*

Rate: 10

- **What did each person say or do?** *"He cheated, broke up with me, and then he posted photos of his new girlfriend. It was upsetting, because my family and friends saw his photos."*
- **How did it make you feel?** *"Humiliated. Betrayed. Hurt. Angry."*
- **How has this person's offense negatively influenced your life? How has this impacted upon your relationship with yourself or others?** *"I am very distrustful of people. I avoid becoming close with anyone. I don't have a social life. I won't allow myself to care about someone again."*
- **What is your relationship with that person like now?** *"We don't have contact. I blocked him on social media."*
- **Are you waiting for an apology?** *"I'm not sure. Maybe an apology would help me to forgive him. But, on the other hand, I don't want to see or talk to him again."*

STEP 5: WRITE A LETTER

This step involves writing a letter (*not to be mailed*) to each person on your list.

Uses your answers to the reflective questions, and refer to the two examples (in the fourth step) as guides.

STEP 6: RELEASE EXPECTATIONS

We all have expectations of others. One common expectation is the desire for an apology, when someone has offended us. When we have been hurt, we want to hear some indication of remorse. The words "I'm sorry," or, "Please forgive me," become so important to us. And yet, very often, we are not going to hear them. Moreover, if we did hear these words, would this truly change the impact that these offenses had upon our lives?

Aside from an apology, we all want and expect to be treated the way that we treat others, yet this doesn't always happen. Everyone deserves to be treated with respect. If someone continually disrespects us, we have every right to exit from that relationship. Nonetheless, this can be complicated concerning relationships with family members or bosses, where we cannot simply sever ties without consequences.

In all relationships, particular expectations can create difficulties, especially the expectation that our forgiveness must be contingent upon an apology. There are people who will not apologize, and they refuse to accept the responsibility for hurting someone. Often, these individuals live their lives blaming others, and see themselves as nothing less than perfect. That's on them, not you. When we stop expecting what others cannot or will not give us, there is a great sense of freedom. Until we truly understand this, we will remain frustrated, because we are powerless over the behavior of others.

If we want to move forward and heal our hearts, our forgiveness cannot be contingent upon receiving an apology. In waiting for an apology, we are giving away our control to the very person who hurt us. More importantly, while we wait for something that will possibly never happen, life is passing us by. This step is simply a reminder that forgiving is for *us*, and it does not require any input from the offender.

Perception vs. Reality

Reality is subjective. It is based upon how we perceive the events and the people around us. You and I can experience the same situation quite differently, and perceive the same people in different ways. That doesn't mean that one of us is right, and one of us is wrong. It just means that we have differences in our perceptions. There is so much power in our perceptions, because they influence our feelings, and how we interpret what others say or do.

Time

Keep in mind that your current stress is primarily due to the hurt feelings, the negative thoughts, and any emotional or physical discomfort associated with the offense. You are dealing with the residual fallout. The original incident might have happened ten years ago, but your feelings cannot recognize that time has passed. When you are re-living an event every day of your life, there is no concept of time, because the intensity has not waned. Therefore, be kind to yourself. Allow yourself to feel the negative emotions that rise within you, and understand that, as far as your heart is concerned, this incident happened yesterday.

STEP 7: IDENTIFY THE LEARNING OPPORTUNITY

In one way or another, everything that happens in life is a learning opportunity, even though it might not feel that way at the time. In this step, list one or two lessons that you might have learned as a result of this situation. Perhaps you have learned about the importance of setting clear boundaries. Maybe you have learned to be careful about trusting someone, until they have earned that trust. At the very least, you have learned that the offender's behavior was unacceptable, and is not behavior that you wish to emulate.

Reminders

Forgiveness is not about condoning that individual's actions. In forgiveness, you seek the peace and the freedom that includes letting go. Recognize that your current primary distress is primarily due to your hurt feelings, not from what happened to you ten minutes or ten years ago. This simple reminder is valuable in helping you to put the situation into perspective.

During this process, when you begin to feel upset, practice stress management to soothe your body's stress response. You might have an urge to stop, and walk away from this process. You might feel that re-hashing old pain is simply not worth it.

Please encourage yourself to honor your commitment. You will get past the different parts of the process, and you will be glad that you did. Take a few deep breaths, meditate, take a walk outside, say a prayer, or do whatever helps you to relax.

STEP 8: CHOOSE TO FORGIVE AND LET GO

This empowering step is about making the conscious choice to forgive. We need to remind ourselves that we are ready to forgive for *our* benefit.

Deciding to forgive includes extending a pardon to the person who has hurt you. Essentially, you are releasing the debt you feel that they owe you. You are also taking your power back, and letting it go for your own sake, so that you can move forward in your life without this burden and distress.

An essential part of forgiveness is *letting go*. We cannot completely forgive and move forward, if we are not willing to let go of our resentments, the past, our obsessive thoughts, our defenses, and our self-righteous indignation. The process of letting go affords us a level of freedom that we cannot experience any other way. What do we lose? Our anger, our resentments, our self-pity and our victim stories. But... we gain our self-respect, our integrity – and ultimately, ourselves.

STEP 9: PERFORM THE SYMBOLIC RITUAL

Visual symbols and rituals can be extremely helpful. After completing all of the steps for each person on your list, gather the paperwork, tear it into shreds, and throw it into the garbage. If you have a fireplace or a wood burning stove, feel free to set it on fire. This visual symbolism enhances the empowering act of completely letting go.

Avoid the temptation to retrieve the shredded list, tape it back together, and keep it. Instead, re-commit to letting go, and remind yourself that forgiveness is solely for your benefit. You deserve the life-changing benefits inherent in forgiveness. Keep in mind that each moment spent in the clutches of a resentment is wasted. And the clock keeps on ticking.

CLOSING THOUGHTS

I embraced certain resentments for two decades. During that period, it felt as if I was carrying the weight of the globe on my back. The emotional pain and hurt that I experienced was horrendous. In hindsight, if I had a time machine, I would go back and change this in a New York minute. Wasted time. Wasted energy. Wasted hours, that surely could have been put to better use. 175,200 hours, to be exact!

Since forgiving and letting go can be very difficult and trying, sometimes these steps need to be repeated, if the offense was severe. Chapter 18: Mindfulness Exercises and Meditations, contains forgiveness meditations that can offer you further support, and assist you in overcoming some of the unyielding obstacles that are blocking your path.

By the way, have you tossed away your paperwork, or set it on fire?

Do you feel like a burden has been lifted?

Allow yourself to fully feel the sense of freedom and the feeling of release within you. It's difficult work and you deserve credit.

Enjoy this feeling…

Envision giving yourself a big hug! You deserve it.

If you need to walk through the steps again, in order to completely forgive someone on your list, that's okay. Practice can help to soften the heart…

9

FORGIVING YOUR SIBLINGS

"Getting along with siblings is not an insurmountable challenge. It doesn't require a miracle, but it might require determined and persistent effort."

OFTEN, IT CAN BE MORE DIFFICULT TO FORGIVE family members, than friends or acquaintances. This is especially true regarding brothers and sisters, since these relationships have been overshadowed and greatly influenced by our history together, as well as possible unresolved issues from the past. In order to have a healthy relationship, each sibling must be willing to openly and honestly address the unresolved issues, work through them, and place them where they belong – in the past. Forgiveness is an important part of this process.

According to a survey conducted by Oakland University, 5% of siblings are estranged, and 16% describe their relationships as adversarial. Troubled sibling relationships are often the result of unhealthy childhood roles in the family, or unresolved childhood rivalry. Another study suggests that 3% to 10% of adult Americans have completely severed ties with one or more siblings.

Aside from a shared history, we have inherited specific childhood family roles, and old patterns can be difficult to break. These do not simply dissolve because we are now adults. They are ingrained and powerful. Past events can strongly affect our present relationships, and add further complexity to our forgiveness work.

In the following interviews, we will explore the complexities and challenges concerning sibling relationships, struggles concerning forgiveness, and possible resolutions. Some of those whom I've interviewed needed to sever ties, some decided to limit contact, and others have chosen to reset boundaries and remain in their relationships.

DIANNA'S STORY

Dianna shared some interesting insights concerning her relationship with her twin sister, Melissa. They were very close prior to their teenage years, then they began to grow apart, as they pursued different interests. Gradually, their dislike for one another grew stronger. Now, as adults, they seem to disagree on every topic, and they are constantly bickering. Dianna admitted that both she and her sister can be opinionated and obstinate at times, and this personality clash doesn't help.

Dianna maintained, *"Today, I would never choose Melissa as a friend. We disagree on just about everything. I guess since we are both stubborn, this doesn't help. The only thing that we have in common is DNA, and a shared family history. I know this sounds horrible, but I just don't like her at all."*

This situation presents an interesting dilemma. Just because you share a family and a history, this does not necessarily guarantee that you will automatically like you siblings as people. What then?

Since several interviewees have shared similar scenarios, this situation isn't as uncommon as it might seem. Years ago, this thinking was frowned upon. Family was important, and if you disliked one of your siblings, well… that was your problem. You were expected to stuff these feelings, and maintain civility and tolerance, for the sake of the family. Today, as a result of cultural changes, individuals are more open about these feelings. This does not, however, reduce the complexity of the situation.

Are you in a similar situation? Is your sibling someone that you would not choose as a friend? Do you share any common interests aside from your shared history? Do you feel guilty about the negative feelings that you have toward your brother or sister?

The more important question is this: Can you or should you maintain a relationship with a sibling, even when you have grown to dislike each other? Only you can answer this question. Before doing so, I would strongly suggest that you seriously think about what your life would be like without your sibling.

If you have answered this question quickly, or based upon anger, then I would suggest that you have not given this question the consideration that it deserves. If, after careful contemplation, you feel that you cannot, should not, and choose not to remain in the relationship, then you have every right to make this choice. Before doing so, however, it might be helpful to read the rest of this chapter, and the insights of others, before taking action.

I believe that it is possible to maintain a relationship with a sibling, even if it requires limited contact. Moreover, I think that salvaging sibling relationships are worth the effort. After all is said and done, it is my belief that family is important. Studies have actually shown that those who have strong family ties or a strong support system, tend to live longer. Shared family history and shared experiences are both powerful bonds.

With some exceptions, getting along with siblings is not an insurmountable challenge. (Unless they are violent, where self-protection is the priority.) It doesn't require a miracle. It does, however, require determined and persistent effort. In the work world, we are able to accomplish this in our relationships with our co-workers on a daily basis. We might not particularly like some of them, but we maintain a level of civility and tolerance. We follow unspoken rules, and avoid volatile or controversial conversations. We do so with ease, because we have to earn a living, and we must adapt. Although family relationships can be more complex and emotionally charged, we have the ability and the skill-set to make adjustments and avoid conflicts.

GREG'S STORY

Greg and his brother have not been on speaking terms for five years. He shared:

"My brother Dave has always been envious of me because I completed college and I have a well-paying job. He had the same opportunity, but he dropped out of college, and he works as a truck driver. Every time I visited him, he would comment about how I was lucky and I got all the breaks in life. His jealousy is ridiculous. Dropping out of school was his choice, and had nothing to do with me."

"The last time we saw each other, he began his usual rant again. I thought to myself, 'Every holiday, I get a knot in my stomach because I feel obligated to see him and his family. My wife and kids get upset, and another holiday is ruined. I can't keep doing this.' "

"The next time we spoke, I confronted him, and said, 'Dave, every time we get together, you make biting comments about how my life is better than yours. This ruins the holidays for me and my family. I just can't do it anymore.' He got angry and denied it, so I cut the conversation short. I haven't spoken to him since. I don't like the situation, but I just couldn't take it anymore."

In response to the question, "Have you forgiven him?," he said: "Honestly, it took a while. The only way I can forgive him is to stay away from him. There are times when I miss him, but I need to put my wife and my kids first."

SHANNON'S STORY

Shannon wrote to me, concerning her sister. Here are some excerpts:

"The last few times that I spoke to my sister, our conversation drifted to the past, and she brought up our teenage fights, and how it still bothered her that my mom would always take my side. We are both in our thirties, and she's stuck back in time."

"I have asked her to stop bringing up the past, but in recent years, the conversation kept going there. I got tired of it, so I began to avoid her. Now, we rarely speak, but we still send each other Christmas cards. Isn't that ridiculous? I don't have a grudge, I just feel badly that we have drifted apart. As much as I want to talk to her, I don't want to argue or keep defending myself. I'm not happy that it has to be this way."

Greg and Shannon are both dealing with the repercussions of sibling rivalry and childhood jealousy. I feel sympathetic towards both of them, and I hope that some day they will be able to resolve their issues. Sibling jealousy creates so many problems that can follow us into adulthood. At some point, we need to let go of these childhood issues, and close the door to the past.

HEATHER'S STORY

Heather, who has five sisters, shared this:

"Our cousins are always arguing with each other. They were very close when they were young. Now, they still act like bratty little girls, and try to pull the rest of the family into their arguments. It's crazy."

"We [her and her sisters] keep our conversations on current events – whatever is going on in our lives now. It's never a good idea to bring up the past, because we can't go back and change things. We also don't gossip about our other sisters behind their backs. This will only lead to trouble."

Heather and her sisters are following the winning formula for success (and her cousins are great role models for how *not* to behave.) Heather and her sisters keep their focus in the now, so childhood issues aren't regurgitated. They have also agreed to avoid creating disruption by gossiping about one another. Since they all respect these boundaries, they can have healthy adult relationships with one another. (I love happy stories.)

BRIANNA'S STORY

"My brother Matt has always been short-tempered. But since his wife left him, he's gotten much worse. He calls me for support, and I try to listen. But, when he tries to justify his actions (being unfaithful to his wife), I refuse to agree with him. Then, he vents his anger by yelling *at me. He's also very angry because he wants me to talk to her, and convince her to return to him. I refuse to do this. He cheated on her, and he was caught. It is not my place to interfere. Dolores (his ex-wife) is a very sweet woman, and I can understand why she left him."*

"I love my brother, but he is getting more abusive with each conversation. Then, we stop speaking to each other for a while, but I always give in and contact him. In a way, I'm mad at myself, because I keep giving in."

First and foremost, if your sibling is violent or abusive, your first priority should be to protect yourself physically and emotionally. No one deserves to be treated this way. Unless or until the situation changes, the healthiest option is to walk away from this relationship, and forgive your sibling.

BENDING AND BREAKING

Brianna and a few others have spoken to me about their inclination to overlook offenses, give in, or assume the blame, in order to keep the peace with their siblings. This deserves further discussion.

My mother-in-law was a very sweet and kind woman. She would often say that sometimes we need to overlook poor behavior to maintain family harmony. She believed that some petty quarrels were simply not worth the effort. In most instances, unless the family member is abusive, I definitely share this view. Sometimes, however, it can be difficult to answer the questions, "How important is this?", and "Should I relent on this particular situation?"

In the movie, *Fiddler on the Roof*, Tevye struggled, but eventually forgave his two daughters, for choosing their own spouses without the help of a matchmaker, thus breaking tradition. When his third daughter eloped and married outside of the faith, he painfully struggled, but could not bring himself to forgive her, saying: *"If I bend this far, I will break."*

Some sibling relationships are so emotionally charged, that they can push you to the breaking point. If you are the type of person who consistently relents in the name of peacemaking, you might eventually feel that "bending" has its limits – and you have reached your limit. Continually backing down is unhealthy. It can steal your self-respect, and create further resentments.

The best way to approach this situation is to have an honest conversation, with some basic ground rules. Avoid judgments or finger pointing. As soon as we begin to blame, the other person stops listening. Use words like "I feel," rather than "You did." Share how it makes you feel when your sibling yells at you or is inconsiderate. Some people have absolutely no idea how their words affect others. If you tell them without blaming, they will be more inclined to receive your words. In sharing your feelings, this will be an important step in re-establishing your boundaries.

If your brother or sister isn't open to having a heartfelt conversation, then perhaps limiting contact might be a way to avoid further difficulties. As mentioned earlier, if the aforementioned options are unsuccessful, then the last resort would be severing ties.

ELIZABETH'S STORY

Elizabeth is a Special Ed Teacher, and she also volunteers at the local animal shelter. She has a very calm demeanor, and is soft-spoken. She and her husband, Frank, have been married for twenty years, and they have a *"great relationship."* Frank is also a teacher.

Her sister, Claire, is a stay-at-home mom, and Claire's husband, Charlie, is a cable technician. Elizabeth asserts that, *"Charlie has always had a drinking problem, and becomes boisterous when he's drinking. According to my sister, he can get abusive when he drinks too much."* Claire has openly expressed jealousy toward her sister, especially since Elizabeth has a good relationship with her husband. As Claire became more unhappy in her marriage, her unprovoked arguments with her sister have increased. Elizabeth has been avoiding her sister's calls, and has considered severing ties.

Scapegoating happens when an individual re-directs their negative feelings onto someone other than the culprit. Nobody deserves to be placed in this role. If this situation continues and boundaries continue to be disrespected, then forgiveness with limited contact might the healthiest option.

INHERITANCE ISSUES

After speaking to several interviewees, I have learned that many sibling estrangements involve inheritance issues. Being disinherited can be heart-wrenching. It feels like the ultimate rejection. One interviewee said, *"It felt like my mother send me a message from the grave, saying that she never really loved me. It has been years, but I never quite got over this."*

In the book, *Overcoming the Inheritance Taboo*, psychologist, Steven Hendlin does a brilliant job in discussing the emotional fallout that occurs between brothers and sisters, when an inheritance favors one sibling. Hendlin talks about how powerful final wishes and words can be. The *will* symbolically summarizes what the parents felt toward their children. Since the siblings are also going through the grief process, emotions are already intense, and sensitivity is heightened. Therefore, there can be a resurgence of past sibling conflicts.

AMANDA'S STORY

Due to an inheritance issue, Amanda has been estranged from her brother for fifteen years.

She shared, *"As hard as I tried, I just could not get past my anger toward my brother. Then, one day, I received a phone message. He said that he was recently diagnosed with cancer, and this caused him to look at his life. He said that he wanted to talk to me and work things out. I was shocked to hear his voice on my answering machine."*

"For three weeks, following his phone call, I couldn't get this message out of my head. I kept thinking about our last conversation. Fifteen years ago, he said he felt he was entitled to my mother's inheritance,

because he took care of her during the last year of her life; even though she told him, in my presence, that he should share her money when she passed, and he agreed. Since she didn't have a will, and her money was in a joint account with him, there were no legal options. After our last heated conversation, he changed his phone number, and we haven't spoken to one another ever since."

"Needless to say, his recent call stirred up these feelings again. I was carrying this grudge for so long. I felt that his actions made it clear that he valued the money more than having a relationship with me... Yet, he was ill now, and he wanted to talk to me."

"I still felt hurt and disappointed. Before this happened, I was always there for him when he needed support, or just someone to listen. I guess that I felt unappreciated. I also expected more of him. I would have handled things much differently."

"I thought about how close we were, as children, then as adults. We always had each other's backs. Honestly, I missed him. Finally, after much thought, I decided to contact Brian, and we met. As soon as we saw each other, we both burst into tears. He expressed his remorse for the way in which he handled the situation. He apologized, and he said that he missed me. Well... long story short, I forgave him. We are back in each other's lives."

Amanda mentioned appreciation and expectations. We all want to feel appreciated, especially if we have gone out of our way to help someone. Yet, this *expectation* can lead to disappointment and resentments. Also, just because we would have handled things differently, does not mean that others will do the same. Sometimes we need to expect the unexpected, and then, *accept* the unexpected. This can be very challenging.

With the exception of Jesus, The Buddha, Mother Theresa, and Gandhi, who have loved unconditionally, I believe that most of us find it difficult to love without conditions and expectations, even though this is a noble goal to strive toward. At the very least, we all want to feel appreciated. Therefore, when our expectations are not fulfilled, we feel hurt, we become angry, and we develop grudges. These wounds are much deeper when we are dealing with family members, and the estrangement is more painful. We need to ask ourselves, "Is this so important that it is worth losing a relationship with my brother or sister?"

TOM'S STORY

Tom began his story with the words, *"I never seem to learn."* This peaked my attention. He continued , *"I keep lending my brother money, even though he has never paid me back. Then I get mad at him. But I know that it's really my fault. What is wrong with me?"*

Tom keeps doing the same thing, but he expects (or hopes for) different results. He's not alone. In fact, this is a popular topic in twelve-step groups, because we have all done this in one way or another. We tend to repeat the same mistakes, even when we anticipate the same outcome. We keep falling into the same potholes.

We all encounter our share of potholes in life. Some can be anticipated and avoided. Others catch us completely by surprise. And there are those that we see, and yet we still fail to avoid them again and again. How many times have we said, "oops" because we repeated the same mistake, even when we were fully aware of the outcome. Tom's *pothole* is his inability to say "no". He knows that he won't be repaid, but he still continues to lend money to his brother. When he get tired of the hamster wheel, and changes his behavior, his outcome will change.

The first time we trip on the pothole, it isn't our fault. What about the second, third, and fourth times? What happens when we fall into that same pothole again and again. Annoyed with ourselves, we think, "What was I thinking?" The worst part is that we can't really can't blame anyone but ourselves.

This is what Albert Einstein might call insanity, which he defines as doing the same thing, but expecting different results. Why? It's familiar. Habits are hard to break. When we reach a place where we're tired of creating negative consequences in our lives, we get better at avoiding the potholes. There is good news. As we keep falling into the potholes of life, eventually, we learn lessons. The metaphorical *hole* creates *wholeness*.

Here are some proactive steps:
- I make a mistake. I had no way of knowing that this would happen.
- Oops. I did it again. I ignored the warning signs. What's wrong with me?
- Obviously I didn't learn from my mistakes. I saw it coming and I knew what would happen. I'm used to reacting a certain way. Bad habits are hard to break.
- Here comes that same pothole. I'm not going to make the same mistake again. No way! I'm avoiding the pothole this time.

UNHEALTHY SIBLING RELATIONSHIPS:

In this section, I want to explore unhealthy sibling relationships, and some of the glaring signs.

The Relationship is One-Sided. If you are doing all the *giving*, and your sibling is doing all of the *taking*, then your relationship is unhealthy. When we are in this situation, eventually we will begin to feel that we are being taken advantage of. When we allow someone to mistreat us, we will eventually lose self-respect, and become angry with ourselves. More importantly, we will continue to accumulate resentments.

The relationship is abusive, or your sibling responds with ultimatums. If the individual is verbally or emotionally abusive, you might be able to correct this situation with a discussion that includes resetting boundaries. If your sibling is physically abusive, then you need to protect yourself by severing ties. A situation with physical abuse calls for forgiveness without reconciliation.

Your sibling is unreasonable. It is very difficult to have a healthy relationship with someone who will not listen to, or honor your feelings. It can be frustrating to deal with this type of person. If a conversation doesn't correct this situation, then forgive, and decide if boundaries or detachment is the better option.

Your sibling is argumentative, a troublemaker, brings chaos into your life, or causes you to feel anxiety. Most of us do not want drama or disruption in our lives. Life can be challenging enough without the unnecessary, added trauma drama. If your sibling is deliberately bringing disruption into your life, remaining in this relationship is a form of self-abuse. Forgive and run to the nearest exit sign.

Your sibling is critical, or judgmental. Constant criticism and judgments are forms of abuse. Some individuals are quite skilled at disguising their criticisms by explaining, "I was only trying to help." This technique places the blame upon you for reacting negatively. Forgive, reset boundaries, or consider detaching from the relationship.

Your sibling is envious of you. There are some siblings that have major issues with jealousy, and some of this envy might have originated during childhood. Envy and jealousy place that individual in a state of perpetual unhappiness. There will always be people who might possess something that we would like to have. So, jealousy is just an endless road toward chronic discontent.

How vocal is your sibling about his or her jealousy? If the jealousy causes unpleasant conversations or arguments, then you will need to address this situation with an open and honest conversation, stronger boundaries or limited contact. The worst case scenario might involve detaching from the relationship.

UNHEALTHY CHILDHOOD ROLES

There are different types of dysfunctional families. Some parents might have psychological problems, addictions, or a lack of parenting skills. In order to survive, children from dysfunctional families assume certain roles, and sometimes these roles continue into adulthood. Below is a synopsis of these various roles:

The *Caretaker/Rescuer* assumes one or both of the parental roles. This child is forced to be an adult at a young age, in order to survive. Sadly, they are unable to experience the joys of a carefree childhood. These children feel pressured, because they also assume responsibility for all of the family members. As adults, some of these individuals might have a strong need for approval.

The *Hero* is the sibling who is in complete denial. This child appears to be good and responsible. Heroes are able to convince themselves that everything in the family is perfect, and they do not recognize the dysfunction. As adults, these individuals might continue the façade. Sometimes they have difficulties with intimacy and honest relationships. On the plus side, they are often excellent leaders and high achievers.

The *Scapegoat* sees all of the dysfunction in the family, and usually vocalizes this to the other family members. The scapegoat usually gets the blame for any problem that occurs within the family. Sometimes, these children are rebellious and angry. This is because they are frustrated, and they do not understand why no one else recognizes or corrects the dysfunction.

I held the role of the scapegoat and the rebel in my family. In fact, my mom often called me the "problem child", which was deeply hurtful. My childhood role was a contributing factor in my ongoing adversarial relationship with my mom. In addition, scapegoats often have ongoing problems with authority figures, and I certainly did. On the plus side, as adults, these individuals are good problem solvers.

The role of the *Clown* exists to diffuse the intensity of the familial conflicts, and bring humor into a stressful family situation. Some children assume this role to get attention from their parents. Those who adopt clown roles sometimes suffer from underlying depression.

The *Lost Child* wants to hide in plain sight. These children are very passive, quiet, and placating. They never argue, disagree, or rebel. They prefer to be unnoticed, because this affords a feeling of safety. These children want to avoid confrontation at all costs. When *lost children* grow up, they tend to ignore anything that might be upsetting, and might prefer limited social contact.

The *Manipulator* is the last role in an unhealthy family. Manipulators learn to cope by becoming troublemakers. They create disruption among the family members, to get their needs met. As adults, many manipulators have the tendency to be anti-social, and can become bullies.

Keep in mind that human beings can be complicated. Very often, people identify with more than one role, and can see different aspects of themselves in different roles. This is understandable.

CLOSING THOUGHTS

Childhood family roles influence our adult lives and our current relationships with our siblings. Again, history is powerful. Forgiveness and reconciliation are possible if all parties are willing to release these childhood roles, be respectful, and let go of the past. Forgiveness is important for *your* emotional well being.

Here are some tips that have worked successfully for many of my interviewees:

- Mutually agree to abide by certain ground rules.
- Re-establish boundaries, and, if necessary, limit contact.
- Recognize that it's okay to have opposing views.
- Be open to hearing your sibling's point of view.
- Listen, without being defensive. It's an art that gets better with practice.
- Avoid the blame game. This will make any situation worse.
- Consider limited contact before exiting the relationship.
- Agree that some topics are off limits, and honor this agreement.
- If estranged, ask a neutral third-party to moderate the conversation. This should not be a family member.
- And... forgive...

We can't change yesterday's news, and obsessing about it will only damage any chance of having a healthy adult relationship today with our adult siblings. When we are angry, we can act upon impulse, often to our detriment. Severing ties with your siblings has so many repercussions, and this decision should only be visited if all other options have failed.

If both siblings are willing to do the work, I truly believe that most relationships can be salvaged. At the very least, a relationship with limited contact can be achieved. I feel that it is worth the work and the effort. I have a sister, and although we have had our ups and downs, I love her, and I am glad that she is a part of my life.

10

FORGIVING YOUR CHILDREN

"When your kids are hurting, you feel their pain.
You wish that you could feel their pain on their behalf…
Of course I forgave. At the end of the day, she's still my daughter."

WHEN DISCORD EXISTS IN A PARENT-CHILD RELATIONSHIP, it's a sad situation for all involved. Sometimes you can become so overwhelmed by your own pain, that you don't see how it is influencing those around you. Parents have their version of the story, and adult children have theirs. The truth is somewhere in the middle. Although they each feel the chill of emotional and possibly physical separation, they share something in common – disappointment and hurt.

Since I had a difficult relationship with my own mother, I get it. I also know how painful and heartbreaking it was for me during the periods when we were estranged. I am sure that it was difficult for my mother too. Sometimes our stubbornness can be our greatest enemy.

COMMON ISSUES

Since I do not have children, I cannot speak from the perspective of a parent. My knowledge and understanding is based upon my experiences as a daughter, from friends, research, support groups, and interviews with parents, who have courageously shared their stories with me.

When a child is little and they say, "I'm sorry," in their cute little voice, it can be so easy to forgive them. They're so adorable when they're small. But what happens when this same child grows up? You now have a history together. Is it still that easy to forgive? From what I understand, not always.

As your child gets older, sometimes forgiveness becomes more difficult. Now your daughter is a teenager. She looks into your eyes and she lies to you. She says she was with her friend, but your neighbor saw her kissing a young man who seemed much older than her. Your son swears that he was not smoking marijuana, even though you can smell it on his clothing. Your daughter screams and curses at you, and you think to yourself, how did we get to this point?

- What if they crash your car, or criticize you on social media?
- What if they are not interested in your forgiveness?
- What if they believe that you own *them* the apology?
- What if you are deeply hurt, and you really don't want to forgive them?

Regardless of the circumstances, parents – especially mothers – are expected to love their children unconditionally. Since they are viewed as the primary nurturers, they are also expected to forgive their children, regardless of the circumstances. Nevertheless, parents are people too. They can feel disappointed and hurt by the remarks or the actions of their children.

Some of the common situations that can cause rifts in parent-child relationships include the following scenarios.

If a parent had poor parental role models or has unresolved childhood issues, this will influence their parenting. How do you fill the parental role if your parents were not good role models? How do you nurture when you weren't nurtured? How can you give what you have never received? In these situations, parents learn through trial and error. There will definitely be a learning curve.

The parents might impose double standards for daughters and sons. Although this has changed, many cultures still have different expectations and rules concerning their sons versus their daughters. In today's world, however, more daughters are inclined to revolt against this thinking.

Some parents struggle when their children assert their independence. Parents want to protect their children, even when the children become adults. Penny shared, *"I don't care how old my children are, I will always worry about them. They're still my babies."*

Deborah talked about the *empty nest syndrome*. She said that she and her husband had to learn *"how to be a couple again,"* when her children moved into their own homes.

Bob shared that he and his daughter have ongoing battles, because she feels that he is overprotective. He did admit that he tends to be very protective of his daughter.

Just as you might have disagreed with your parents, your children are going to disagree with you. Very often your thinking changes as you learn from life experiences. I am a very different person than I was at twenty or thirty years old. Can you identify areas where you might have changed over the years?

As explored in Chapter 9, sibling rivalries and jealousy can cause a great deal of family tension and resentments. Nearly every family has a child who believes that his brother or sister is being favored and treated differently. There are other children who are jealous of the accomplishments of their siblings. If these situations are not resolved, they will follow us into our adult sibling relationships. In the meantime, they will create disruption within the family.

As children get older and develop relationships outside of the family, sometimes the parents do not disapprove of their child's chosen friends or love interests. If the adult-child chooses a life partner that the parents dislike, this discord needs to be resolved to avoid resentments. Acceptance is the key.

Here are some insights shared by moms and dads who had forgiveness issues with their adult children:

- Accept that you cannot control or fix their feelings.

- Love your children, even though you might dislike their behavior.
- Maintain hope that reconciliation might be possible in the future.
- Respect and accept their choices, even if you disagree.
- Allow them to learn from their own mistakes.
- If your adult child is willing to talk with with you, try to really listen.
- Find someone trustworthy that you can confide in.

EMILY'S STORY

Emily shared that she has two fourteen year old twin boys and a sixteen year old daughter. She said that the most important thing she learned as a parent was patience. *"I love my kids, but sometimes they can really try your patience. And they definitely test you. Boys are definitely easier to raise than girls, but my boys have had their share of injuries from playing sports and trips to the Emergency Room. Girls have different types of problems."*

On forgiving her children, *"There were times when my daughter has gotten angry and has said some hurtful things to me. I told her that I felt hurt, and she has apologized. Of course I forgave her. At the end of the day, she's still my daughter."*

VIVIAN'S STORY

"The relationships with your children are very different from other relationships. When they're small, it's easy to fix their hurt feelings with a kiss or a toy. It's not so simple when they get older. I have a son who is twenty years old. He was dating a girl that treated him badly, but he said he loved her and to mind my own business. We had many arguments about her. Eventually, she left him for one of his friends. He got angry with me, even though I was never rude to her. I think he just didn't know where to place his anger."

"On one hand, I felt terrible that he was suffering because she left him, but I was glad he wasn't being mistreated anymore. If he wasn't

my son, I wouldn't have put up with his anger. When your kids are hurting, you feel their pain. You wish that you could feel their pain on their behalf. Did I forgive him? Yes – without a doubt."

CLOSING THOUGHTS

Eventually, most parents will forgive their children, even when they might not deserve it. Most will concede, even when their feelings have been hurt, and they feel that they were not at fault.

During my interview with Stacey, she told me, *"My daughter wasn't speaking to me for several months. We had an argument, and we both made thoughtless comments. Even though I felt hurt, I wanted to fix the damage between us. So, I went to my daughter's apartment. I was very nervous, because I didn't know how she would react. When she opened the door and saw me standing there, she had tears in her eyes. We didn't say a word, and she immediately hugged me. She invited me in, made coffee, and we talked. I'm glad that I made the first move."*

II

FORGIVING YOUR SPOUSE OR LIFE PARTNER

"Separate your love that you feel toward your partner, from the words or actions that have hurt your feelings."

WHAT ARE THE INGREDIENTS NEEDED TO SUSTAIN a happy, long-term relationship?
It appears that the general consensus points to forgiveness and kindness as the two major contributing factors. To maintain relationship longevity, each partner needs to be able to forgive, compromise, release grudges, and move forward.

According to the National Survey of Family Growth, the U.S. divorce rate peaked at 40% in 1980, and has been declining since then. The probability of a first marriage lasting at least a decade was between 68-70%, while the probability of a marriage lasting 20 years was between 52-56%. (These statistics are based upon marriages, so this information does not include co-habitations.)

Michael Rosenfeld's research focused upon longevity-specific data. This study included 3,000 married, unmarried straight, and gay couples. Here are his findings: most breakups occur within the first two years. Couples who were in a relationship for five years, had only a 20% breakup rate, and after ten years, the likelihood of a breakup decreased even further. The statistics indicate that a long relationship greatly decreases the possibility of a breakup.

All participants agreed that successful relationships don't just happen, they require work and ongoing effort. There are many factors that contribute to making a relationship satisfying and able to stand the passage of time. These include loyalty, trust, honesty, good communication, common interests and goals, and the willingness to compromise. More importantly, we need to be able to forgive, move past our disagreements, differences of opinion, and the inevitable daily frustrations in life. Without forgiveness, ongoing resentments will eventually damage the relationship.

When we harbor grudges, we create an atmosphere of underlying tension, where even a small disagreement can escalate into a domestic war. In this state, we are easily triggered, and our anger can cause us to amplify the negative, and ignore the positive. If we want to move past our relationship hurdles, then we need to talk to our partners, share our emotional pain, possibly re-establish new boundaries, and let go of offenses. If we are in the wrong, then we need to apologize. Another important ingredient is to separate the love that you feel toward your partner, from their words or actions that have hurt your feelings.

My spouse and I have different opinions on certain topics. Like all couples, we have our moments where we can get annoyed with one another. We also have joyful moments, and after over four decades, I can still laugh at his jokes. Most importantly, at the end of the day, we are best friends.

INTERVIEW HIGHLIGHTS, FINDINGS AND SUGGESTIONS

Several couples in long-term relationships were interviewed, and they were asked the question: What are some of the secrets that have helped you to maintain a long term and a happy relationship? Here are some of the responses and repetitive themes. Notice that the responses reflected kindness and forgiveness.

THE BENEFIT OF THE DOUBT

It's very easy to misinterpret comments. (Refer to the chapter: *Communication Contamination*.) If we have other stressors, they can amplify misunderstandings. Seek clarification before escalating an argument based upon presumptions. If you're unsure about the intent of a comment, give your partner the benefit of the doubt. Don't automatically assume the worst.

THE POWER OF THE PAUSE

Pausing during a heated argument can de-escalate it. When you pause, you have time to calm down, compose yourself, gather your thoughts, and process what your partner is saying. Then you can respond, rather than react.

ROLES REVERSAL

Put yourself in your partner's place. Let's say that your partner is angry, because they are jealous that someone was paying attention to you. They interpreted this as flirting. Below the surface of their argument, you might realize that their reaction is just a sign of insecurity. Have you ever felt insecure or jealous? Be honest. Would you want forgiveness and reassurance? Reversing roles can help you to understand the other person's point of view and underlying feelings.

REFLECT UPON THE POSITIVE

When we have been deeply offended, we focus on the hurt and pain. All else eludes us. If you are trying to forgive a comment or a behavior that has hurt you deeply, it might be helpful to balance the scales. Write down the reasons why you love the person who has hurt you. Then write down the positive aspects of your relationship. After you have weighed the pros and cons of the other person and your relationship, you can address their particular offense with balanced insight.

BE COGNIZANT OF TRIGGERS

We all have particular characteristics that we dislike about ourselves. If our partner makes a comment related to our Achilles' heel, it can lead to an argument. Sometimes, even an innocuous comment can be misinterpreted, especially if we are overly sensitive to this particular character flaw. In that case, it might be helpful to explore why the comment triggered such a powerful response. Your reaction might be more about your hypersensitivity, than your partner's comment. In any case, you need to forgive your partner, just as you would want to be forgiven.

POUTING AND CHILDISHNESS

When you refuse to forgive your partner, and insist upon clinging to your anger and resentment, you are behaving immaturely. This is a form of control. Visualize a little child holding their breath because they're not getting their way. It might be cute when you're a child, but it's not very endearing when you're an adult.

We have all behaved childishly at times. When you feel upset, you want your partner to be upset, too. One way to accomplish this is by not accepting their apology or refusing to forgive them. If you are playing this game, reverse roles. How would you feel if your partner refused to forgive you? Put on your grownup hat and do the right thing. You will feel relief when you do so.

TAKE THE HIGH ROAD.
(THERE'S USUALLY LESS TRAFFIC UP THERE).

Have you ever been in a horrible mood, where every little thing annoyed or irritated you? If you were in a pleasant mood, however, this same comment might not have bothered you at all. In these moments, you need to overlook the comment, and forgive your partner. Sometimes we need to choose our battles wisely. Take the high road, and let it go.

BE UNDERSTANDING AND TOLERANT

We each have a personal style of communicating. Just as your partner or spouse can annoy you at times, it is likely that you also have some qualities that your partner finds annoying. Besides this, you simply might not agree on different issues. If you are passionate about an issue, tolerance for opposing opinions can be very difficult. Believe me, I know. However, you can learn to respect differences, even when you don't agree. Tolerance... not always easy, but achievable.

OWN YOUR PART

If you want to resolve a disagreement, you will need to look at your part in contributing to the problem. (Yes, I understand how difficult this can be when you're angry). Take a few deep breaths, have an honest talk about the situation, compromise, and agree upon a plan to fix the problem. Blame or retaliation only escalate a conflict. Do you want to be right, or do you want to be happy?

LEAVE THE PAST, IN THE PAST

Sometimes, when we disagree with others and become angry and defensive; we bring past offenses into the conversation. This is especially true if we believe that we might be losing the argument. In fair fighting, we agree to keep the focus upon the current issue. It is counterproductive to address past offenses that have already been resolved. This will only escalate the argument. Also, two sentences that should be excluded from every argument are: "You always..." or "You never..." Be fair, focus upon the current discussion, and avoid regurgitating the past.

DON'T GO TO SLEEP, WHILE STILL ANGRY

It is impossible to get a restful sleep if you are angry. Your body is in a heightened state of anxiety, and your thoughts are working overtime. If you are lucky enough to fall asleep, you will open your eyes the next morning, and feel the same anger and upset that you felt the night before. It's important to resolve the conflict with your partner before going to bed.

A few of my interviewees presented this scenario, and it is share-worthy: What if you go to sleep with unresolved anger, and your partner doesn't wake up the next morning? Do you find this thought disturbing? Consider that it is always a possibility. If this happens, it is likely that you will not be unable to forgive yourself. How important was that heated argument now?

COMPROMISE

Every successful relationship includes compromise. In long-term relationships, however, we might forget this. Sometimes, we begin to take our partner for granted, and become insensitive to their feelings. A healthy relationship includes sacrifice and compromise.

NOBODY EVER REALLY WINS AN ARGUMENT

If you are more concerned with winning the argument than resolving the problem, then both you and your partner lose. Do you really want to win a battle that leads to losing the war? Nearly every problem has a mutually acceptable solution, when we are able to place our egos aside.

DON'T USE THE SILENT TREATMENT

This is a passive-aggressive way to punish your partner, and it only makes a bad situation worse. First of all, it takes a lot of effort and energy to be silent when you are angry. By being silent, you are actually hurting yourself. Beneath the silent, cold exterior, is a brewing volcano. As angry as you might be, the healthier part of you wants to resolve the situation. It's better to talk about your feelings than avoid a conversation. Sooner is better than later.

FORGIVING AFTER THE DEAL BREAKERS

Are you still struggling with unresolved resentments, anger, and hurt, following a divorce or breakup? Here are some suggestions:

- Stop recycling the anger by repeating your victim story.
- Convert your negative experience into a list of lessons that you have learned.
- Focus on those things that you can control – your attitude and your thoughts.
- You cared about your partner once. Acknowledge your disappointment and hurt.
- Divorce or ending a relationship doesn't mean failure and can be the start of a new beginning.
- Invest your energy in working toward forgiveness rather than retaliation.
- Adopting a forgiving perspective will help to alleviate the repetitive cycle of pain.

A divorce or the end of an intimate relationship can result in strong feelings of resentment, sadness, failure, disappointment, anger, sorrow, and fear. If you have children, this further complicates the situation, because you will continue to have some contact with your ex-spouse after you part ways. Forgiveness will help you to move from the position of victim to survivor, and will alleviate the stress in your future interactions with your former partner.

CLOSING THOUGHTS

From time to time, every relationship will face challenges. At the very least, we are going to have disagreements or might become complacent. The important thing is how we approach and resolve these hurdles. Regardless of the circumstances, forgiveness is the key to the success in every relationship. This is true, whether or not reconciliation is a viable option.

12

FORGIVING YOUR PARENTS

"Making peace with our parents is the epitome of forgiveness."

"WHY CAN'T SHE BE DIFFERENT?" This was the ongoing question I had about my mother when she was alive. It never occurred to me that she might have had this same question about me.

Looking back... after I forgave my mom, and recognized that she was an imperfect woman, (just like me), I was able to see that I could have saved myself a lot of grief if I understood this when she was still alive. At that time, I could not see past my disappointment in her (and perhaps she could not see past her disappointment in me, as well). This disappointment led us through long periods of time where we did not speak to one another.

As a part of my forgiveness work, I had to see the world through my mom's eyes, from the position of an adult woman, rather than a wounded child. As I did so, I was able to fully understand how difficult and stressful her life actually had been. More importantly, I was able to recognize that, despite her shortcomings, she was a very courageous woman. Although we were not blood-related, (more about that later), I have certainly *inherited* her courage and resilience.

Making peace with our parents is the epitome of forgiveness. Often, we will need to let go of a lifetime of hurt and disappointment, rather than a single incident. Although it requires a great deal of work, it is worth the effort. If we can fully forgive our parents, the others on our forgiveness list will pale in comparison.

Whether we realize it or not, many of our problems with other people are in some way a reflection of our unresolved issues with our parents. These fractured relationships influence our relationships with our life partners, spouses, friends, employers, and even our children. Moreover, these unaddressed conflicts can often cause us to have adversarial feelings toward authority figures such as teachers, police, and employers. Obviously, this can create a lot disruption in our lives. Yet, beneath every angry rebel is a disappointed, frightened, and wounded child.

Like all of us, our parents have also been shaped by the remnants of their history, their struggles and their stories. Up until now, you have probably viewed your parents through the eyes of a wounded or disappointed child. Understanding each of these aspects will take you closer toward forgiving them, as you learn who they are (or were), through your eyes as an adult. This is why writing their story is such an important step.

The process of writing my mother's story was very powerful. For the first time, I felt her struggle and her pain. I was able to see her as an imperfect woman who had to deal with many difficult obstacles. Although our life circumstances might have been different, I was still able identify with her some of her struggles, and especially her feelings.

I devoted a great deal of time writing, rewriting, and reflecting upon my mother's story. It's amazing that with each revision, I was able to understand her on a much deeper level. I am sharing her story and my reflections in fairly great detail, because I am hoping that perhaps my thoughts and sentiments will resonate with you, and help you when you write your own narrative during this step.

You will notice that my mom's narrative/story is much longer than my dad's. In part, this is because of the intensity of unresolved feelings I had toward her, and partly because she was the same-sex parent, and she was very influential in my life. Moreover, my dad died when I was a teenager, and I don't have many memories of him.

MY MOTHER'S STORY

My mother was a beautiful woman with blonde hair and blue eyes, and she looked exactly like her mother. She loved jewelry, and always made sure that she looked her best, even though she had a lot of medical problems, and she struggled with her weight.

She was first generation American, born of Italian immigrants, and she was bilingual. When she didn't want us (my sister and I) to know what she was saying, she spoke to my father in Italian, who was also bilingual. Yet, neither one of them had an Italian accent.

My grandfather was a hardworking brick mason, and my grandmother was a homemaker. My grandmother was also a very sick woman, who suffered from severe hypertension. Sadly, she lived during a time before blood pressure medications existed. Still, she was a loving mother who took good care of her family, and she was fondly remembered by her children and my grandfather.

My grandmother went to the afterlife at the young age of forty-seven, and although my grandfather was a young widower, he never remarried. From what I was told, my grandmother was a sweet and kind woman. She loved nurses, because she was chronically ill, and she was grateful for the loving care that they gave her. Therefore, she and my grandfather saved what little money they had, so that they could send one of their daughters to nursing school.

I know that my mom never quite recovered from the premature death of her own mother, because she often spoke about her mom, and how much she missed her. I'm sure that this loss has an enormous impact upon her life and influenced her role as a parent.

Like many parents during that era, my grandparents were strict with their children. My mother often shared this story concerning a curfew she had when she was a teenager. She went on a date and saw the movie *Gone with the Wind*, but she had to leave before the movie was over, since her curfew was at 10 pm. It always bothered her that she never saw the end of that movie.

One day, I noticed that the movie was scheduled to be on television, so I watched it to the end on her behalf. It wasn't my favorite movie, and it was very long, but I watched the entire movie in honor of her, and her unfulfilled wish to see it to its conclusion.

My mom was married at the age of nineteen. From what I was told, she and my father really wanted children, but there were difficulties in conceiving. I have heard stories that my mom would often cry, because she desperately wanted to be a mom. After ten years of marriage, since they felt that they would not be unable to have biological children, they adopted me. Then, two years later, my mother became pregnant, and she gave birth to my sister.

And then, something happened that changed my happy parents. Through the eyes and the memory of a child, I remember that there was a great deal of stress and friction in our household. Within the last few years, I learned new information that offered some additional insights.

I recall ongoing discord between my parents. I did not know the specific details, but I did know that they were constantly anxious about finances. Due to gambling issues with my father, which led to serious financial difficulties, my mother was eventually forced back into the work force. This was very difficult and stressful for her, because she had many medical issues, including rheumatoid arthritis and a heart condition. Despite this, she went to work every day.

Although my mother went to high school, she did not have work-related experience, so she could not find a white collar job working in an office. The only job that she was qualified for was that of a seamstress. She was a very talented seamstress, and she had a talent for crochet and knitting as well. To make ends meet, in her spare time, she would also crochet and knit beautiful items, and sell these locally.

Working as a seamstress was far from a glamorous job. The

working conditions were atrocious. She worked in a sweat shop, doing piecework. This meant that she was paid for each piece of clothing she assisted in making. Added to the stress of being paid by the piece, there was no air conditioning. Can you imagine being in a room with twenty to thirty women behind sewing machines, in the brutal heat of the summer? Not pleasant. She was an intelligent woman, and her arithmetic skills were amazing. She could add and subtract numbers in lightning speed without calculating the sums on paper. Sadly, I am sure this was not the life that she had envisioned for herself.

When my sister and I were teenagers, my father became seriously ill and passed away. The survivor social security benefits were minimal, and he did not have life insurance. Ultimately, my mom was forced to sell our house to pay his enormous hospital bills, and we had to relocate to a three-room apartment. Consequently, we had to discard many of our belongings. Can you imagine moving from a house into a small apartment? It was a very upsetting time, filled with sorrow, fear, uncertainty, and numerous adjustments.

At the young age of forty-seven, my mother must have been a very frightened widow. She was now solely responsible for raising two teenage daughters, we could barely make ends meet, and she must have been terrified about the future. It's interesting to note that my grandmother died at the age of forty-seven. I think that, in many ways, as my mother's world began to crumble, a big part of her died at the exact same age as her mother. Sometimes you can still be alive, but you begin to feel that you have lost pieces of yourself, and this feels like a form of death.

My mother could be somewhat stoic at times, she had difficulties in expressing affection and she hid her feelings. It was easier for her to express anger and frustration, rather than hurt or disappointment. Now I can see that this was a form of self-defense – a way to protect herself and her vulnerabilities. At times, she did show her more sensitive side, and would share that her feelings were easily hurt.

It was after her death, when I learned that my dad wasn't the role model husband that he portrayed himself to be. Additionally, he had his own unresolved issues that resulted from a very sad and abusive childhood. In lieu of these new insights, I was able to understand why she shut down emotionally, after being hurt and disappointed a number of times. Nonetheless, she was always loyal to my father, and she never spoke badly about him or betrayed his trust.

FAST FORWARD... LIFE WENT ON...

Although I was married, we seemed to continue our periodic battles at a distance. We argued and bickered about nonsense, as the days quickly turned into years. Since we both had a tendency to be obstinate, this make our relationship more contentious.

Then, when I was forty years old, I accidentally learned that I was adopted. This shocking revelation was a bombshell, and it placed more stress upon our relationship. I felt that I had been deceived, and I was not interested in hearing her side of the story. From my perspective, everything that I thought was true was actually a lie. Eventually we reconciled, but the confusion that I felt concerning my identity lingered on for quite some time. (See the later part of this chapter for further details.)

When my mom was seventy-three years old, she had a cerebral hemorrhage, had unsuccessful surgery, and was in the hospital for seven weeks, before she went to the afterlife. There was a lot of confusion and family disruptions after her death, but the details are unimportant now. And, although we had our disagreements, we got along much better during her last few years.

POST-FORGIVENESS THOUGHTS AND INSIGHTS

After my forgiveness work concerning my mom, my life and my

feelings have drastically changed. Once upon a time, I would feel anxiety when she phoned me, because there was the possibility of a disagreement, and we both became defensive with one another very easily. *Now, I would give anything to hear her voice just one more time.*

Today, and every day, I look at her photo, send her love and light in the afterlife, and tell her that I miss her and I love her. I truly do miss her with every fiber of my being. I have always loved her, but couldn't get past the walls between us. Sometimes I mourn the loss of what could have been – the possibility that we could have had a better relationship, one without friction or power struggles.

We could have done so if both of us had let down our guard for a few seconds, to see the other person as an imperfect woman, rather than a battle to be fought and won at all costs. In this sense, we were more alike than different. Alas, there aren't any time machines or magic wands. We cannot change the past, but forgiveness will change our future.

And so, I forgave her for not being the mother that I wished that she could be, and I forgave myself for intentionally making her life difficult at times, because she couldn't live up to my expectations. I also forgive her for other issues. Through the forgiveness process, I was able to understand that some of her actions were in response to her own hurt and feelings of rejection.

Now, when I look back and think about her life, I see that she was a very brave and courageous woman. Although the odds were against her, giving up was never an option. Was she perfect? Of course not. Who is? Did she make some mistakes? Yes. Nevertheless, to this day, when my life gets difficult, I remember her words, "You have to give yourself courage. No one can do it for you." These words continue to give me strength when I'm going through rough patches.

As you can see, these games that we play in response to our resentments, are a vicious cycle. It is a battle that no one will win. These battles can continue indefinitely, unless we break the cycle and adamantly refuse to continue. Someone has to reach into their *Higher Self* and say, "For heaven's sake, this is insane. Enough is enough!"

Whether your parents were the best, or the worst parents in the world, you will probably miss one or both of them when they're gone. I can tell you from my own experience, that if your parents leave the physical world before you are fully able to forgive them, your unresolved resentments will probably eat away at you like the worst type of acid, until you have forgiven them.

As mentioned at the onset of this chapter, we are addressing a broad scope when dealing with resentments toward our parents. This makes forgiveness more challenging and complicated. Please know that your heart will gradually heal when you allow yourself to let go and forgive. I had to do a lot of work to get to this place, and the journey was painful and liberating at the same time. When I completely forgave my mother, I felt incredible relief.

I hope that this sharing helps you to see that you are not alone. So many of us have issues and grudges toward our moms. Our maternal relationships are distinctly unique. This is why unforgiven resentments towards our mothers can cause us the most grief.

Are you ready to begin the process of forgiving your mother? Let's get started...

STEP ONE

The first step is to write your mother's story, and capture a glimpse of her world through her eyes. If you don't know all of the details, that's okay. Just do the best you can. I want to clarify that this exercise is not about condoning any wrongdoing. It is about creating a new level of understanding, by seeing the world as she might have seen it.

Keep in mind that there's a possibility that your mother didn't get what she needed from her own mom. Her mom might have been emotionally or physically unavailable. Perhaps she feels some of the same disappointment in her mother that you have toward her. She might have a needy and unforgiving inner child too. At some point, someone needs to break the cycle, and understanding is the first step.

After you complete this step, wait at least twenty four hours, and then re-read what you have written. Before you do so, I would like you to pretend you are reading a story about someone you do not know. You will be surprised at how much insight you gather as you read her story again.

The next step is to write down all of your pain, hurt, and disappointment, and all of your needs that you feel she did not meet. You can glance at the partial list that I have provided, and check off what might resonate with you.

Here are some common areas which might require your forgiveness:

- All the ways she wasn't there for you.
- Not spending more time with you.
- Not being more loving.
- Not recognizing your achievements.
- Not supporting you and guiding you.
- Any abuse or neglect.
- Criticisms and verbal abuse.
- Addictions.
- Mental illness.
- Being weak.
- Being insensitive or stoic.
- Not being a better spouse to your other parent.
- Not taking the time to understand you.
- Not protecting you.

Here is a question to reflect upon, before continuing with the steps: Do you believe that anyone can live up to all of these expectations?

Next...

STEP TWO

This step is about having an imaginary conversation with your mom. Place two chairs facing each other about four to five feet apart. If you have a photo, place it on the empty chair where your mother would be sitting. If you don't have a photo, this is okay. You will just need to use your imagination, and bring forth a mental image of her.

Imagine your mother sitting in the empty chair. Look into her eyes...

Imagine that you are able, just for a few moments, to see her as simply another person – a woman, who might have had her own struggles in life...

Listen to her, as she puts down her guard, and shares her fears... her insecurities...her own wounds...

Listen to her as she tells you that she loves you... how she made some mistakes...

How she tried her best, in spite of her limitations... in spite of her own hidden pain...

Hear her say that it was never your fault... that you were her beautiful child...

How she wishes that she could take away all of the pain that she caused you...

How she wants to understand how you feel...

Now open your heart and share your hurts, your disappointment, your anger...

Look into her eyes again... you see tears in her eyes, as she says: "Please forgive me."

If you feel inclined, imagine giving her a hug – if not, that's okay too.

Now go to that place deep down inside you, where you feel love and compassion...

And take the first step toward forgiving her...

MY FATHER'S STORY

My dad's story is much shorter than my mom's story. One reason for this is that he passed away when I was a teenager, and I have some gaps in terms of my memories concerning him. Here is his story, to the best of my reconnection…

My father was also of Italian-American descent, bi-lingual, and the son of immigrants. He was forced to assume the role of breadwinner when he was nine years old to support his family, because his father has issues with authority figures, he wasn't in love with the idea of working for a living, and he was unable to keep a job for very long. My father's childhood was very unhappy and short-lived.

It is my understanding that he was the victim of child abuse by both parents. There were times when his parents locked him in a closet for days, and punished him by refusing to feed him. Despite this, he was always respectful to his parents, and he never expressed any overt resentment toward them. He probably repressed all of his anger, hurt, and disappointment, which resulted in stomach ulcers, other stress-related illnesses, unhealthy, and passive-aggressive behavior.

During his childhood, he discovered that the woman who he thought was his mother was actually his "stepmother." He learned this from neighbors, but he never told his parents that he knew this information. Apparently, my grandfather left his wife and his other children, and took my father, who was his eldest son. He relocated, and at some point, he met my grandmother. If my father didn't learn this information, he would have continued to believe that his step-mother was his biological mother.

My father spent his entire adult life wondering about his birth mother and his other siblings. According to my mother, not knowing about his birth mother and his biological family always troubled him. And yet, he never confronted his parents concerning this issue.

Upon my grandfather's death, my grandmother moved into our house. She was very intrusive, and had boundary issues. Her presence increased the tension in an already somewhat turbulent home, and the arguments between my parents increased. She remained in our home for a couple of years until she passed away.

Unlike his dad, my father was not lazy. He was a baker, and he worked twelve hour days, six days a week. On Sunday, he had a second part-time job for a couple of hours. The ovens were extremely hot, and the work area did not have air-conditioning. This job required a lot of energy, because the bakers were expected to prepare and bake a large volume of bread. Like clockwork, he went to work, came home, and went bowling every Wednesday.

My father's childhood experiences were very damaging, and he was left with many unresolved issues, which led him to high-risk, damaging and unhealthy behaviors. He also had a huge gambling problem that nearly cost him his life. He hated the idea that he worked so hard, yet could barely make ends meet. Like all of us, he wanted more out of life, and saw gambling – and the hope of winning – as his only option. This was a perfect storm for disaster.

Since he didn't want my mom to know about his gambling problem, he made the mistake of borrowing money from the local loan sharks. One day, two well-dressed men in three-piece suits came to our home, while my dad was at work. I still remember that day, because I overheard the conversation, and it terrified me.

I heard one man politely say to my mother, "You know, it would be a shame if there was an accident, and something terrible happened to your husband, or to you or your children. We don't want to see that happen. We just want to be re-paid, so we can resolve this situation." My mother was completely blindsided. She had no clue that this was happening. She was extremely upset, so you can imagine the scene when my father came home.

To resolve the situation, and to protect our entire family from harm, my aunt and my uncle intervened and loaned my parents the money. My mother had to return to work to help repay the debt. She also monitored the finances, and he never gambled again. Nevertheless, this situation created overwhelming burdens and stress, and I'm certain that it damaged the trust that my mom had toward my dad.

Looking at his life through the eyes of an adult, and as someone who has worked in the psychology field, it is clear that my father lived an unhappy and troubled life, filled with pent-up feelings, anger, frustration, sadness, disappointment and low self-esteem. Even so, he presented himself as a happy, carefree, family man, and he desperately wanted to be liked by everyone.

Since I had to forgive my father for some serious offenses, it was difficult. After doing so, however, I felt great relief and freedom. Again, we forgive so that *we* can heal.

NOW IT'S YOUR TURN ...

In this **first step**, write your father's story, and try to view the world as he saw it. If you don't know all of the details, this is okay. Just do the best you can.

This exercise is designed to bring a broader level of understanding to his life.

What was your father's childhood like? What did your father lack in his childhood? What were his parents like? As with your mom, there is also the possibility that he didn't have healthy parental role models, or he didn't get what he needed as a child. Maybe he has some disappointment or hurt related to his childhood. What was his adult life like? What were his possible stresses or insecurities?

Wait one day, and then read his story again.

Now take a few deep breaths...

Feel free to refer to the checklist that I listed earlier, and write down all of your anger, pain, hurts, and disappointment.

THE SECOND STEP

Place two chairs facing each other, and place his photo on the empty chair, if available.

In a quiet, comfortable place, where you will not be interrupted, begin this meditation...

Imagine your father sitting in the empty chair. Look into his eyes...

Imagine that you are able, just for a few moments, to see him as simply another person – a man, who might have experienced his own struggles...

Listen to him as he puts down his guard and shares his fears... his insecurities... his own wounds... perhaps his own struggles with trying to be a good dad...

Listen as he tells you that he loves you... how he made some mistakes... failed...

How he tried his best, despite spite his limitations... and his own issues and hidden pain...

How he tried to be strong...

Hear him say that it was never your fault... that you were his beautiful child...

How he wishes that he could take away all of the pain that he caused you...

How he wants to understand how you feel...

Now open your heart and share your hurts, your disappointment, your anger...

Look into his eyes again. He's hoping that you don't see his tears, as he says...

I am so sorry. Please forgive me... I love you.

Now go to that place deep within you, where you feel love or compassion...

Now take the first step toward forgiving him...

THE LETTER

The letter format is designed to assist you in gathering your thoughts, in preparation for the next step, where you will visualize having a conversation with each of your parents. (Do not mail it.) In the first visualization, your parents were speaking to you, and you were asked to take the first step toward forgiving them. However, it is very important to share your hurt feelings with them, before you can completely let go and forgive.

You will be given this opportunity in the next step.

Here are some additional questions to guide you:

- How has this parental relationship influenced your life?
- How has it influenced your relationships with others?
- In what ways has this influenced your relationship with yourself?

Recognize that what happened was not okay, and allow yourself to feel any negative feelings. When you are ready, write your letters, leading with: *Dear Mom,* or *Dear Dad...*

These steps are painful, yet heart-healing, so have the tissues available. After writing the letter, it should be ripped up or burned. This is the symbolic part of letting go, and it is powerful.

SOME IMPORTANT AFTERTHOUGHTS...

I believe that forgiveness is ultimately a choice. More importantly, it is the only exit door out of the pain-drenched existence of unforgiveness.

You will need to tell yourself that you are ready to forgive for *your* benefit. Make the decision to forgive for *you*. In forgiving, you are releasing the debt you feel that they owe you. You are taking your power back, and letting it go for *your* sake, so you can move forward in life, without this distress.

FORGIVING TWO MOMS AND A DAD...

Before closing this chapter, I want to share one more story, where I had to forgive both of my parents as well as my biological mother. This story deserves further mention, because it was life-changing. The revelation that I was adopted, and the ensuing fallout, required an incredible amount of forgiveness, especially since I was an adult at the time, and for forty years, I believed that I was their biological child.

In addition to forgiving my parents, I had to forgive my biological mother, a woman who suddenly became a key character in my own story. She was someone that I never knew existed – this faceless woman – this stranger. Someone I would not know, even if I bumped into her in a store. Was it intense? Mind-boggling? Overwhelming? You bet it was! Since my father was deceased, and my mother was still alive, she had to deal with my shock and anger alone.

Prior to learning this information, I spent my entire life believing that I had my father's dimples, my grandmother's smile, and my mother's light skin complexion. Try to imagine that you have suddenly discovered that everything you were told about yourself was fabricated. It's an overwhelming thought, isn't it? How do you even begin to forgive this? Gradually, and in layers…

As mentioned above, I was forty years old when I accidentally discovered that I was adopted. I was not intentionally looking for this information, although I have always had a feeling that this might be true for a variety of reasons.

It was a warm summer's day, and I remember being excited that my husband and I were going on vacation to Cancun, in Mexico. Since this would be my first time traveling out of the United States, I learned that I needed either a passport, or a birth or a baptismal certificate as documentation. (The laws have changed since then.) I was rushed for time and couldn't find my birth certificate, so I decided to get a copy of my baptismal certificate.

It was a short drive to the church where I was baptized. Since their files weren't computerized, they were able to retrieve the original paperwork regarding my baptism. Standing in the church office, I showed the receptionist my driver's license, and she spoke to me. Little did she know that a brief, casual conversation would change my entire world.

Assuming that I already knew that I was adopted, the receptionist innocently said, "Oh, so you were adopted." It was not really a question, but rather, a polite attempt to chat. After hearing her words, although my world began to shatter around me, I calmly said, "Yes, I was." I felt my heart pounding like a loud bass drum, but I maintained a calm façade remarkably well. I will never forget the feeling that the ground was crumbling beneath my feet. My legs felt weak, and I felt like a human earthquake.

The receptionist handed me the copy of my baptismal certificate, and graciously began to explain the information. The first line had my given name. Beside it was a second given name in parentheses. She explained that this name (Eleanor) was given to me by my biological mother.

The next lines had the names of my (adoptive) mother and father. Following my mother's name (in parentheses) was the first and the last name of another woman. This name, the receptionist explained, was the name of my biological mother. As she spoke, I began to feel queasy, so I gave her a check for the fee, thanked her, and quickly exited.

Standing on the sidewalk in front of the church, I just stared at the certificate for a couple of minutes. I tried very hard to compose myself, but my thoughts were racing. As I looked at the document, I kept hoping that I either misread it or I would wake up from a very bad dream. Neither happened, and I remained in a surreal state for a couple of minutes.

I got into my car, and my entire body began to shake. I drove home and phoned my husband, who was still at work. As usual, he was very supportive. We briefly chatted, and he said he was coming home from work, and then we could talk about it further.

He asked me to stay calm.

I reflected back to when I was ten years old, and I asked my parents if I was adopted. At that time, I had a vague feeling that I might have been adopted. They showed me the birth certificate, and their names were listed as my parents, so I believed that I must have been mistaken. I did not know about amended birth certificates at that time.

I phoned my mother and told her that I just learned that I was adopted, and I shared the details. She was very upset, and she said she couldn't talk at the moment, and would call me back. At that point, I was not concerned with her feelings. I was overwhelmed with my own shock.

Apparently, she phoned my aunt, because the phone rang, and my aunt told me that this was very upsetting to my mother, and she felt that this could cause my mother to have a heart attack. I felt that she was attacking me, and she wasn't considering my feelings, or how upsetting and shocking this was for me. In hindsight, I guess she was just trying to protect her sister.

I ended this conversation abruptly, because call-waiting indicated that my mother was phoning me again. We were both still upset, and I wanted an explanation and information. She was livid that I was given this information. Later, I learned that she had wanted to take this secret with her to the grave. It took years for me to understand why she might have felt this way.

After speaking with her, I decided to look through my Baby Book, since this is where the lies began. I read the entry which said that I had dimples like my father. (Years later I learned that my birth mother also had dimples), my mother's smile, and I resembled my grandparents. The baby book created a story that biologically connected me to my adoptive family. Perhaps this was wishful thinking from my mother's perspective.

I guess that as the years went on, more lies were created to validate other lies, and this made the situation very complicated. I think that it reached a point where there was no turning back. Since I was rebellious teenager, I believe that perhaps this increased their fears of telling me the truth.

Some time passed after my first conversation with my mother. I wanted an explanation but I was so angry, that nothing that she could say would have helped me to feel better. Still, I listened to her explanation. My mother told me that she and my father made a decision not to tell me that I was adopted, because they didn't want me to feel unwanted. She said that they really wanted a child and she had difficulty conceiving. She felt blessed that she was given the opportunity to adopt me.

Now, I can understand this to a certain extent. Back then, I simply could not see beyond my own overwhelming pain, and my anger blinded me from seeing her pain. It took a long time before I was able to consider and understand her reasons and her feelings. My mom is in the afterlife now, and sometimes I still wish that we were both able to hear each other's point of view.

I want to point out that this occurred during a time when people thought very differently. Over the years, society and ideas have changed, and I am happy to see that parents tell their children that they are adopted. It's not as shocking when you learn this at an early age.

Coming to terms with the fact that I was adopted took quite a while. There was a lot to forgive: the lies, my identity, and my resentments toward my parents and my biological mother. Even though my mother explained the details surrounding my adoption: (my birth mother was very young, she struggled with this decision and she wanted me to have a good life), I still struggled.

It took quite a while to get past what I considered to be deception. I also felt abandoned and rejected by my biological mother – a complete stranger. My mom and I had difficulties in our relationship already, and this certainly didn't help things. I began to wonder, "Do I look like my birth mother?" and "What was she like?" For some reason, I wasn't very interested in knowing about my biological father, but I was extremely curious about my biological mother. Eventually, I forgave my parents and my biological mother, but the forgiveness happened over time, and on different levels.

During times of pain and struggle, I have always found it healing to express myself with words, and I wrote this letter to my birth mother, several months after learning the truth.

A LETTER TO MY BIOLOGICAL MOTHER (TO THE WOMAN I NEVER KNEW)

I wonder how you felt about giving me away... Did you ever wonder about me or think about me? Now, I think about you... Sometimes I miss you, although we've never met, especially when I'm feeling like a scared little girl again.

You have missed the most important moments of my life. Did it matter to you?

Sometimes it matters to me... At times I wonder if you would have been proud of me. I guess it really shouldn't matter now, because you're not here, and I'm getting too old to keep searching for a mother.

I have always felt a void throughout my life – a vague sense of infinite emptiness – a missing piece of a puzzle. At least I now understand why that hole existed.

Still...when I'm feeling vulnerable, I can't help but wonder about the mother I never knew.

So, until we meet again, please know that I forgive you, and maybe we will meet in heaven.

Years later, I am able to fully understand that she was in a difficult position, and she placed me for adoption with my best interests at heart. It was a painful and perfect act of selfless love and sacrifice.

I also understood that, as the years went on, it became harder for my parents to tell me the truth. My mother explained that she wanted me to feel that I was a part of the family. She was afraid that I would not be able to handle this information, and I would have been devastated if I learned the truth. She didn't want me to feel that I had been abandoned. I was a very sensitive child who reacted to situations very deeply and intensely. My parents, knowing that, made a decision to take this information to the grave. I understand this now.

Today, people are more open and share this information with their children. During my childhood years, information concerning adoption was more secretive and taboo. I don't doubt that I might have been devastated if I was told this as a child. I think, though, that I was meant to discover this information. Eventually, I re-grouped and moved forward.

THROUGH THE EYES OF A CHILD

Before closing this chapter, I feel that it's important to present some final insights that helped me to forgive my parents. Please reflect upon these three questions, before you read the remainder of this chapter.

- Do you see the world differently now than you did ten years ago? How about twenty years ago?
- Do you believe that you saw the world differently as a child?

When we are children, all of our experiences are filtered through our developmental level at that time. We try to understand our world and the actions of others through the eyes of a child. As we mature, hopefully, we begin to view life differently. Nevertheless, our childhood memories have been etched in our brains from a child's perspective. Moreover, some of our memories might be lack clarity due to the passage of time.

When we transition from childhood to adulthood, we don't close one door and open another. Then, voila' – we are now 100% adult and 0% child. Some individuals never grow up, they just grow old. The rest of us are floating somewhere on the child-adult spectrum. Many of us tend to approach our painful childhood memories through the eyes of the child we once were. This doesn't invalidate any of the pain we might have experienced in our childhoods. It is, however, worthy of a closer look.

As an adult, I returned to my childhood neighborhood. In my childhood memories, the house appeared to be gigantic.

Viewing that same house as an adult, it looked so small. I was really surprised at the difference between my recollections and the reality. My perception was tainted by my perspective as a child. This old memory, however, was crushed to dust, after I saw this house through the eyes of an adult.

And my point is? Perception is subjective, and not always 100% accurate, and our resentments can taint our perceptions in powerful ways. This point is worth reflection and consideration.

Before I forgave my parents, I was only able to remember the painful and hurtful memories. Unfortunately, there were quite a few that followed me into adulthood. It was interesting, however, that I could not recall one pleasant memory. As the resentments melted away, however, I began to remember many of the happier memories. This insight showed me that grudges can block our ability to see the entire picture.

Even if we were abused, mistreated, or neglected, each time that we re-live the pain of yesterday, we are losing each moment of today. More importantly, we are engaging in abuse by proxy. The culprit – the proxy – is us!

CLOSING THOUGHTS

Resentments are in love with expectations. It keeps them alive. Once you wave goodbye to your expectations, it will be easier to forgive and release the resentment. Our primary expectation is usually the desire for an apology from our parents. We believe that hearing remorse will soothe our pain. The last thing that we want to hear is "I did the best that I could," when we feel that their "best" simply was not *good enough*.

Consider this… *Maybe,* just *maybe,* it *was* the best that they could do, given their limitations, their own unresolved wounds and issues, and the resources that were available to them at that time.

If you are still struggling to completely forgive, consider reading their story again, and try to see and feel what it might have been like to live their lives. This process is not meant to find excuses, but to discover explanations.

Then, ask God, your *Higher Self*, or the universe, to strengthen you and allow you to see beyond the accumulation of disappointments that you have gathered over the years. Tell the wounded child within you that they're safe now. It is time to let go of the disappointment and live your best life. Close your eyes and try to envision the shadowy glimmer of the rainbow, that is peeking out behind the clouds. Reach up and envision yourself touching the colors of this magnificent rainbow.

As mentioned previously, some people are incapable of apologizing. They will not assume the blame. They think that apologizing and admitting that they were wrong mean that they are less of a person. It is even more difficult for parents to look at themselves. In apologizing, they are essentially admitting that they have failed. It is a huge admission. They have difficulties in conceding that they might not have been a good parent. At the very least, they were not the parent that you wanted, needed, and expected. That's one enormous apology!

If you want to move forward and heal your heart, then your forgiveness cannot be contingent upon receiving an apology. The moment you stop expecting, you will be able to complete your forgiveness journey and your life *will* get better.

I carried my childhood resentments toward my mother into my adult life. These unresolved grudges tainted and placed stress upon my adult relationship with her. Since we were both strong women, this didn't help the situation. If you are in this place, and your mom is still alive, then I urge you to attempt a woman-to-woman conversation with your mom. If this helps, you will save yourself much grief and pain. If you cannot work things out, then at least you know that you have done your best.

What about reconciliation? Reconciliation is a personal choice, and it depends upon your particular circumstances. This is discussed in greater detail in Chapter 17: Releasing Relationships. If your parent fails to respect your boundaries, or is behaving abusively, then you might need consider forgiveness without reconciliation. If your parent respects your boundaries, then, by all means, forgive and reconcile.

13

FORGIVING CHRONIC OR SERIOUS ILLNESSES

*"Adversity illuminates life's deeper meaning,
It can soften our hearts, and helps us to become
more understanding of others, and receptive to forgiveness"*

It can be very challenging to live with a chronic, progressive, or serious illness. These life-changing situations can stir up many feelings that will need to be worked through. In this chapter, we will explore the various aspects of forgiveness, as these relate to medical issues. Since I have kidney disease, as well as chronic pain from other medical issues, this chapter is very important to me, and it is my hope that, if you are in a similar situation, it might help you as well.

If you are living with a chronic or a serious illness, there is a good chance that you have experienced a wide gamut of emotions. You might feel anxiety, a sense of loss, fear, anger, frustration and sadness. Besides feeling unwell, you might also need to adjust your diet, your lifestyle, and your social life. Your medical situation could require ongoing treatment, hospitalization, or surgery. It wouldn't be surprising if you have developed resentments toward your illness.

In this chapter, we will explore these questions:

- How do you overcome this type of resentment?
- How do you forgive an illness, as opposed to a person?
- How do you address and come to terms with this type of challenge?

In *Man's Search for Meaning*, Holocaust survivor, Dr. Viktor

Frankl, shares important observations and insights. Some of these can be applied to those who live with chronic, progressive, or serious illnesses.

- Even though our freedom or our possessions can be taken from us, no one can take away our freedom to choose our attitude.
- When we are powerless to change our external circumstances, we are forced to focus inward, and change ourselves. This includes our perception of our situation.
- In the midst of pain and adversity, we can still find our meaning and purpose in life. Moreover, doing so can greatly influence our healing.
- We must forgive in order to achieve and maintain mental health and recover from our wounds, especially our emotional wounds.

When faced with serious health challenges, initially, we might feel very sorry for ourselves. Honestly, who wouldn't? This is completely understandable. "Why me" is a normal first reaction. We might even vacillate between moments of self-pity, and periods where we feel composed and more accepting.

At some point, we need to accept our circumstances and assume a proactive stance toward our health management. (And, we don't need to like something in order to accept it.) If we allow ourselves to drown in self-pity or remain paralyzed by anger and resentment, then we are giving our illness permission to control us.

After we accept that which we cannot change, we will be more open to learn about our illness, get in touch with our inner strength, and take charge of our treatment options. Eventually, we might be able to help or inspire others who are faced with similar challenges.

Coming to terms with a serious medical challenge includes an evolution of the heart. Once you understand your situation on an intellectual level, you need to accept your circumstances at the heart level. Before beginning the work of forgiving your illness, you need to mourn your losses. As you progress through the stages of grief, you will able to identify and process your feelings.

The grief process is not linear. You might take a few steps forward, and then slip backward. Despite the forward and backward movement, if you do the work, you will eventually progress through all the steps on the grief path. Hopefully, with time, you will choose to use your experiences as a way to reach out to others in similar situations.

Both myself and some whom I have interviewed found that helping others was very heart healing and gratifying. Moreover, through time and introspection, many individuals have also shared that their circumstances offered them an opportunity for personal growth and empowerment. They recognized that they were much stronger than they ever realized.

If you are in this situation, there will be times when you think, "What's next?", "When?" and "Will I be able to handle it?" Most people who are diagnosed with chronic or serious illnesses, initially react to the news with alarm, as they replay the doomsday scenarios in their minds over and over again.

Honestly, I did this when I first recognized all the repercussions of moving from kidney insufficiency to chronic kidney disease. I cried, I blamed myself, and I felt the full intensity of the fear associated with the eventual treatment options and lifestyle changes associated with this particular disease. Then, I regrouped, and began to follow the renal diet, I lost weight, began to take vitamin supplements and did a lot of praying and meditating.

Over this past year, while I was writing this book, my kidney function declined, and I was told that I needed to be on dialysis. I am updating this chapter to reflect my current circumstances.

On the same day that my veterinarian told me that my basset hound needed emergency surgery, (which was very upsetting, because my animals are my fur children), my nephrologist told me that I needed to be on dialysis. (Talk about Murphy's Law!) I have to say that if I didn't believe in God and the power of prayer, and if I didn't believe everything in life is an opportunity for learning and growth, I would have crumbled. But I did not. And that, in and of itself, is miraculous.

Within the next few weeks, I will be having surgery, and by the time you read this book, I will be on peritoneal dialysis, with the hope of eventually getting a donor kidney. Considering my current situation, I feel fairly well, with some increased symptoms associated with this disease, like itching, tiredness, and nausea. I am told that the dialysis will help. Nonetheless, I did need to grieve a new set of losses, and, once again, forgive my illness. Even though I knew that this was coming, it still shook me.

As I mentioned before, my mother would often say that we have to give ourselves courage, and nobody can do this for us. Reminded of these words, I took a deep breath, regrouped, drew upon my inner strength through prayer and meditation, and I decided to make a conscious effort to stay in the now.

I reminded myself that I have been through so many other obstacles in my life, and yet, here I am – still standing. I have always been resilient, and have survived situations that would have brought many to their knees. Giving up has never been an option. I am a survivor and a warrior.

As a result of many hours of meditation and prayer, I believe that God, the archangels, and my mom in heaven, assisted me in getting in touch with my inner strength. I also believe that nothing in life happens by accident. A few days before I was presented with this news, a friend and I were talking about angels and archangels, and because of her suggestions, I began to pray to Archangel Raphael and Archangel Michael. Raphael helps with illness, and it is believed that he has "the medicine of God", and Michael protects us from harm and fear, and has an army of angels to assist him. It has been decades since I've prayed to angels, in addition to my prayers to God. Coincidence? No way.

In addition to spiritual help, no one can underestimate the power of love and support. It helps to have someone who will calmly listen to our feelings and our fears. I am so blessed to have a spouse who is kind, understanding, my best friend, and my greatest supporter. So, now... I'm okay with these new circumstances. Not thrilled, but okay. (Thank God I haven't lost my sense of humor.)

I believe that our bodies are greatly influenced by our spiritual and emotional states of mind. I know that worrying just adds more stress to an already challenging situation. My life style will change, but I have control over my attitude and how I approach the *new normal*. Daily, I also make a conscious effort to keep my thoughts in the present moment, rather than thinking about what tomorrow might bring. This is very helpful in relieving stress and alleviating fears based upon projections.

I have also re-focused my attention, by doing tasks that I enjoy. *I stopped putting everything in my life on hold, to be revisited at a future date.* I continue to meditate and pray daily. This helps me. If you have other ways that work for you, it's all good.

I have also joined a support group, where others are dealing with the same medical issues. I am also reaching out to support others in this group. It always helps me to direct my efforts toward helping others, because there is always someone who is hurting and could use some support. The best way to dissolve feelings of self-pity is join a group, and offer encouragement to those in need. There are so many support groups on social media sites.

THE NOTION OF TIME

Your concept of time, as well as time management, will change when you live with an ongoing illness. As you move past the initial shock, and fully grasp your circumstances, you come face-to-face with your mortality. At this point, you will begin to see time differently. Every moment becomes valuable and you begin to use it more wisely.

Before my diagnosis, like many others, I lived my life under the illusion that I did not have an expiration date, and I procrastinated. Often, I didn't finish the projects that I so enthusiastically began. Now, I am far more self-motivated and self-disciplined. Some of those whom I have interviewed for this chapter, have also shared that they don't procrastinate the way they did before.

THE PRELIMINARY WORK

There are similarities between forgiving a *person* and forgiving an *illness*. At some point, you need to exit the mental battlefield, make peace with your circumstances, forgive and release any resentments, identify the learning opportunity, let go, and move forward. However, as mentioned above, forgiving an illness includes grieving your losses. These include the physical and the psychological challenges that are a part of your particular illness.

THE PATH OF GRIEF

The new limitations imposed by your illness, will create a sense of loss, similar to that which is experienced from the loss of a loved one. For instance, you may find yourself unable to engage in certain activities that you once enjoyed. You may lose friends, because you might be unable to make plans in advance. If you don't know how you will feel from one day to the next, making plans can be difficult. Since life becomes challenging and frustrating, it can become very easy to develop a grudge.

Let's take a look at the stages of grief, as they apply to chronic or serious medical situations:

SHOCK AND DENIAL

When you are first diagnosed with an illness, you might react with shock, followed by denial. These defense mechanisms protect you from becoming overwhelmed, by softening the intensity of the reality. Denial initially alleviates the shock of the frightening news. Denial can also make you believe that your diagnosis is incorrect.

EMOTIONAL PAIN AND GUILT

As the shock and denial subside, pain and sadness rise up. You need acknowledge and experience the sadness so that you can transcend these feelings. Helplessness is a horrible feeling, and knowing that you cannot change a situation requires a great deal of acceptance.

As you grieve the loss of your physical health, you might begin to blame yourself. You may think, "I should have done this," or, "I shouldn't have done that." Self-blame and guilt will only increase your distress and lead you into a deeper state of despondency. If you learn that you might have contributed to your illness, you need to forgive yourself. If your medical condition was unavoidable, then you need to acknowledge that some situations are simply out of your control. I do understand how difficult this can be.

ANGER AND BARGAINING

Feelings of frustration and powerlessness can fuel your irritability, leading you to become short-tempered with your loved ones. Although anger is a part of the grieving process, you need to be aware of how your reactions affect your family and friends.

Unchecked, your anger can damage your relationships, and alienate your greatest allies and supporters. Remember, your loved ones are also upset about your illness and the emotional pain that you are experiencing.

You can relieve your frustration by talking to someone that you trust, seeing a counselor, or joining a support group. Often, within every angry person is a frightened little child. Getting in touch with this inner child can help you to understand yourself on a deeper level, and shed the armor of anger.

You might resort to *bargaining* after exhausting all other options. Bargaining can include prayers such as: "Dear God, I will do x, y and z, if you heal me," or "Dear God, if you make this illness a misdiagnosis or a lab error, then I promise to be a better person." Another form of bargaining might include doctor shopping. This includes gathering second opinions from other physicians, or seeking additional medical opinions, hoping to learn a different or a more hopeful diagnosis.

REFLECTION AND DEPRESSION

At this point, all of your defenses have melted away. You recognize that guilt is pointless, and bargaining cannot change the situation. You also realize that anger only exacerbates your discomfort. Alas, there are no barriers between you and your situation. As you reflect upon your new reality, you might become depressed. Some individuals are more inclined to isolate and avoid social contact, even though this increases their loneliness.

In facing the reality concerning my own medical issues, I felt like I was in a small rowboat being tossed about by stormy waters. Even though I had a strong support system, I still felt frightened and isolated. It helped me to reach out to my Higher Power (God) for comfort and spiritual resilience. I still use prayer and meditation as valuable tools in helping me to maintain inner strength, balance, and insight. Please utilize whatever works best for you.

THE LIFE ADJUSTMENT STAGE

In this fourth stage, your life will gradually take an upward turn. Depression will begin to dissipate, as you become more comfortable, and you adapt to your lifestyle changes. One day at a time, you will adjust to your new challenges, and reorganize your life accordingly. We can do anything for 24 hours, and this concept has helped me to deal with every single challenge in my life.

ACCEPTANCE AND HOPE

Acceptance and hope are the final stages of the grief process.

Acceptance does not mean that you have to be happy about your circumstances. It just means that you stop kicking and screaming, and gracefully accept what you cannot change. During this period, you will begin to take charge of your life, adjust, and carry on.

INTERVIEWS

Several individuals with chronic illnesses were interviewed on the topic of forgiveness and the grieving process, as it relates to medical illnesses. Although their illnesses have caused limitations in their lives, most viewed themselves as empowered survivors. They believed that their medical challenges allowed them to better support and assist others. They also saw a connection between the lessons they have learned (due to their medical challenges), and their capacity to be more sensitive, understanding, and forgiving of others. Here are some of their stories.

ERICA'S STORY

Erica lives with chronic pain and discomfort due to degenerative disc disease, fibromyalgia, and arthritis. Prior to these medical issues, she was very active, and enjoyed camping, skiing, and traveling. However, as her symptoms became progressively worse, and were further exasperated due to an auto accident, her activities deceased significantly. She shared:

"I was very angry and resentful at first. My life went from being very active, to practically a halt. I was upset with myself, because as hard as I tried, my pain was so overpowering, and it prevented me from doing the things that I loved. I take medications, but these only help to a certain degree. I didn't know where to direct my anger and my sadness. It took a long time before I could forgive my limitations and my illnesses."

"I had to re-invent myself and my place in the world… Actually, I had to re-invent who I was as a person. I also had to find replacements

for the activities that I can't enjoy anymore. I went through a period of mourning, similar to when my mother died – a feeling of emptiness and loss."

"I felt so helpless and sorry for myself, and I wanted to blame someone or something. For a while, I was not easy to be around. After a while, I realized that I had a big grudge because of my illness, the constant pain, all of the losses, and my new, limited life."

"I joined a support group, and they told me to make a gratitude list. I wasn't happy about that, but I wanted relief, so I tried to do it. I began with the basics. I had a place to live, financial security, food to eat, and people who cared about me."

"I shared this with the group, and a group member suggested that I add one more item to my list. She said, 'You have the gift of today.' For some reason, those words spoke to me. I began to realize that today is really a gift. None of us know what tomorrow will bring. We have this day, and we get to decide how we want to live it."

"Then, I took the leap, and reached out to help others. Some were sicker than me. As I started to talk to these women, I learned that they didn't see themselves as victims. They came to terms with their illnesses and they didn't feel angry or resentful. They helped me to forgive my illness. Rather than being upset, I began to use my experiences to help people, and I became a stronger and a better woman. Gradually, my anger and resentment melted away."

"Grief? In looking back, I guess you can say that I went through different stages of grief – shock, denial, anger, and mostly self-pity. It took a while to accept things. Now, I have adjusted to the changes, and I try to think about the good things in my life. Things that once seemed so important are less significant now. I can see that I am stronger than I ever realized. Sometimes this still surprises me."

MARGIE'S STORY

Margie co-owns and manages a restaurant. She has three adult children who live locally, she has been married for twenty-two years, and she and her husband Danny, own a home which is located quite close to the restaurant. She's very charismatic, witty, and articulate, and she has a story worth sharing.

Knowing the topic before we spoke, she began by sharing, "*If you don't forgive your disease and make friends with it, then it will control you and drag you down. You need to take charge. I have chronic kidney disease, hypertension, and diabetes. I take my medicine religiously, watch my diet, and do peritoneal dialysis at home. Other than that,*" she laughed, "*I feel terrific!*"

She continued, "*Every day, I tell my kidneys that we're a team. I will take care of them [through daily treatment], and they need to take care of me, by working their best. I know this might sound odd, but it helps me to feel that I'm in control of my health. It helps me to keep my mood upbeat.*"

"*When I was first diagnosed with kidney disease, I was already being treated for my high blood pressure and diabetes. The mere thought of this disease is frightening. Then, in a very short period of time, it became progressively worse. I needed to learn how to do the home treatment. I was frightened by the unknown and I felt depressed.*"

"*After reading a magazine article about people who talked to their diseases, I gave it a try. I told my kidneys that I was angry with them. Then, I realized that it was ridiculous to be fighting an internal war with myself. I had to befriend my kidneys. I guess you could say that I had to befriend all the aspects of myself – the good and the bad. I'm on several lists, and I am hoping for a kidney transplant. I understand that there are more kidneys available now since they found a cure for hepatitis, and I'm hopeful.*"

"*Danny helps me a lot. He really stepped up. He has a lot of patience and always lends a listening ear. My kids live nearby, and we're close. I can't tell you how important it is to have a supportive family.*"

"*Regarding your question, about forgiving my illness: I guess you could say that I forgave my kidney disease. I don't feel anger or self-pity anymore. Physically, I feel much better since starting the dialysis. Since I am in a few support groups, I hear a lot of stories. I've learned that everyone faces struggles in life. This is mine.*"

Since I have kidney disease too, Margie's words were very encouraging and inspiring to me. We chatted further, and we have kept in touch. We speak to each other often.

DANNY'S STORY

When someone we love is living with a serious illness, it also affects us. Danny is married to Margie, and he wanted to share his story too.

"It was very frustrating to hear that my wife had such a serious illness, and it progressed very fast. She's a vibrant woman, and it was upsetting to see her so frightened and sad. We're very close, and she shared her feelings with me every step of the way. I'm so glad that I can be there for her."

The denial was first. She wanted to get a second opinion, and I think that this helped her to confirm that she needed the dialysis. I went to the classes with her, and I think that it helps her to know that I'm in her corner and want to help."

"At first, she had her ups and downs. It was definitely a roller coaster ride. After a while, she became more comfortable with the treatment. She does the dialysis in our home while she's sleeping, and she looks a lot better now."

"I think that if it was me, I couldn't have handled as well as she did. She's one brave woman."

CLOSING THOUGHTS

Margie mentioned internal battles... we all have them. And yet, we can't win a battle when *we* are our *own* opponent. To overcome the challenges inherent in chronic illness, we need to exit the battlefield and resolve our resentments, educate ourselves, bravely accept our circumstances, and become proactive in our care.

When you are faced with a chronic or a serious illness, this significantly changes your outlook on life. Sometimes, your life becomes more meaningful. You might feel grateful for the little things that previously escaped your awareness. You may appreciate your good days and come to value the importance of living in the now.

There are many similarities between forgiving a person and

forgiving an illness. At first, you might feel victimized and angry. With time and reflection, you can learn and understand more about your illness, and move past any feelings of resentment. Although you cannot control or change external circumstances, you have complete control over your reactions and responses. This is where your true power lies. Acceptance helps to elevate your moods, relax, and respond from a position of empowerment.

All in all, we are often more resilient and adaptable than we realize. That which does not destroy us, truly makes us stronger in every way. As we become emotionally stronger, we begin to look toward the future while enjoying our lives from this new perspective.

Adversity often illuminates life's deeper meaning. It forces you to challenge yourself, to learn new skills, and to come face-to-face with your courage and your resilience. Challenge can also help you to be more sensitive to the needs of others, to soften your heart, to be grateful, and to be more open to forgiveness.

14

FORGIVING SEXUAL ASSAULT AND CHILD MOLESTATION

*"The past has weighed me down too long.
Today I'm choosing a new song."*

Sexual Assault

AMY IS THE TYPE OF PERSON THAT MOST PEOPLE ENJOY being around. She has a terrific personality, she's smart, and she always has a smile on her face. She is a warm and sweet woman, and appears as if she doesn't have a care in the world. In the years that I have known her, she always had a kind word for everyone. One day, we were discussing forgiveness, and I asked her if she thought that there were some offenses that were unforgivable. Amy said that she experienced a traumatic experience that many people would find reprehensible.

During her freshman year at college, she was sexually assaulted by a fellow student whom she trusted. Amy never reported this to the police, and many years passed before she was able to tell her family. Moreover, it took fifteen years before she was able to completely forgive him. Her difficult journey included pain, anger, shame, struggle, and finally, letting go. She explained that she did not do this for his benefit, but rather to alleviate the pain of all the pent-up rage that she was feeling.

Amy suffered with post-traumatic stress syndrome for many years. If she was in a store, and a particular song was playing on the overhead radio, she would need to leave, because she would have flashbacks and an anxiety attack. If she saw someone on TV who resembled the perpetrator, she would panic if she couldn't change the channel fast enough. Regardless of how hard she tried, she simply could not find inner peace, and she lived in constant fear. She avoided intimate relationships, she was terrified of the dark and she was afraid to go out at night.

She had to make a conscious decision to forgive him, because she did not want to continue living her life overwhelmed with fear. She decided against confronting the perpetrator, because he lived thousands of miles away now, and she did not want to initiate contact with him. All of the work was done within her own heart, and with the help of prayer. She found it helpful to write a letter (which was not sent), telling him about all of ways that his assault impacted upon her life.

When she forgave him, and let go of the burden of the resentment, she noticed significant changes within her. She began to go out after dark, and realized that she wasn't afraid anymore. In the past, she couldn't go to sleep unless she had the light on, but now she is able to sleep comfortably in the dark. She felt more comfortable in her relationships with others, began to experience happiness and serenity, and her panic attacks ended.

Sexual assault is one of the most difficult offenses to forgive. Yet, at the same time, forgiveness can be life changing, because it takes the individual on an inner healing journey, from a helpless victim to an empowered survivor. I was quite struck by how, in forgiving, her life changed and improved on so many levels.

According to the National Sexual Violence Resource Center, one in five women and one in sixteen men are sexually assaulted while in college, and 90% of victims do not report the assault. It was shocking to learn how frequently this crime occurs, and that it happens to 20% of female college students. Statistics give us numbers, but they do not reflect the damage and the pain caused by sexual violence.

These statistics were also alarming. One in four girls, and one in six boys, will be sexually abused before they are 18 years old, 34% of the perpetrators are family members, and only 38% of victims report these crimes.

CHILDHOOD ABUSE

There is no crime more reprehensible than child abuse. These horrendous experiences create lifelong issues that touch every area of the survivor's life. Adult survivors often live in a defensive state, and recovery is a slow process that requires a great deal of work. Besides forgiveness, they must grieve the loss of a carefree and safe childhood that they deserved and missed. Many children might not remember the vivid details, while others have vague and fuzzy memories. Many survivors have *body memories* (these are uncomfortable, physical feelings associated with the trauma).

I was molested when I was a child. As a result, I had PTSD for many years. I had clips of images, and particular aromas that were troubling and upsetting. As I put the fragmented pieces together, many of my forgotten memories returned, and I was able to identify one of the perpetrators. This work was painful and healing at the same time. More importantly, it helped me to understand some of the reasons why I struggled with particular feelings and fears.

As a consequence of my own molestation, I shared some of Amy's PTSD experiences. I was afraid of the dark, so I slept with a light on for many years. When I heard one particular song, I would have a panic attack, because this song triggered the feelings, terror, and flashbacks of the molestation.

It's sad that sometimes music becomes associated with our traumatic experiences. I am a musician, and music has always brought joy into my life. Therefore, the idea of feeling terrorized by a song was very upsetting. To this day, when I hear that song, it still sends a lightning bolt of anxiety through my body. However, my mindfulness exercises have helped me to get past this trigger quickly.

Through counseling, I began to realize the full extent of what happened to me, and other parts of my life started to make sense. Counseling was very difficult. I had to re-live the pain, and grief the many losses that this violation created. In hindsight, and through my experiences as a client, and later, as a counselor, I know that only path to healing involves walking through and past the pain, and emerging stronger.

It took a long time before I was able to forgive. Like Amy, I forgave for *myself*. Years later, I learned one of the perpetrators was also a victim of childhood abuse, and from what I understand, he lived his life in a state of denial, and could not come to terms with it. This is not an excuse, but it is an explanation.

In addition to counseling, it was helpful to attend a support group, where I received validation and compassion. More importantly, it helped me to see that I was not alone, and that I was a victim through no fault of my own. With time, I began to see myself as a strong woman and a survivor.

Although I had to overcome many difficulties as a result of this trauma, I have been blessed with inner strength and resilience. Counseling was instrumental in helping me to get to this place. Like Amy, when I forgave the perpetrator, I felt free, and my heart was able to heal.

To clarify, forgiveness has nothing to do with seeking justice through the judicial system. If possible, the perpetrator should be prosecuted and punished for this crime.

Unfortunately, this is not always possible with child abuse crimes that have occurred decades ago. These laws, however, are slowly beginning to change, and some states have eliminated the statute of limitations on these crimes.

If you have been a victim of sexual assault or molestation, please know that you are not alone, and today there is more help available than every before. I know your pain because I have lived it. More importantly, I have transcended the pain and trauma, and grew stronger. So can you. Take your time as you work through the forgiveness steps. Keep in mind that, as Amy said, that you are forgiving the perpetrator as a gift to *yourself*.

CLOSING THOUGHTS

It is difficult to forgive sexual violations. There are painful memories and emotions that must be re-visited and conquered. If you have been victimized, please know that you are a *survivor*. This distinction is important. You have the right to live your best life, and let go of this baggage. You surely don't want this baggage glued to your very being forever.

Forgiveness is not releasing the perpetrator from the responsibility. It is saying: "I refuse to give you the power to make my life miserable anymore. Goodbye forever. I release you, and now, *I am truly free!*"

15

COMMUNICATION CONTAMINATION

"When you consider the complexity involved with communication, it's incredible that we can communicate with one another on any level."

CAN YOU IMAGINE HOW MANY RESENTMENTS could be avoided, if we were more informed, and we had better skills on how to communicate effectively with one another? This chapter will offer you some useful tools and a broader perspective concerning communication. Sometimes, we can avoid communication difficulties by understanding cognitive biases, and how we process words and information. It is also helpful to understand some of the basics of non-verbal communication.

COGNITIVE AND MEMORY BIASES

Cognitive and memory biases cause us to make inaccurate judgments, decisions, and interpretations. Below are some of major biases that contribute to communication contamination.

The Gender Bias might be less prevalent than it has been in the past, but it still exists. Women are still held to different standards than men are. If a man speaks assertively, he is seen as a strong leader. When a woman sounds assertive, she is labeled *nasty, a witch,* or *hormonal.*

The gender bias was very obvious in the past presidential election, where there was a male and a female candidate. The media was more interested in what the female candidate wore and what her make up looked like, then on what she had to say. No one was interested in the male candidate's attire. Sometimes individuals are unaware of this bias, which makes it more insidious.

A confirmation bias is the tendency to favor information that supports our beliefs.

This bias allows us to remember the information that supports our views, while forgetting, misinterpreting, or distorting opposing information. We hear what want to hear, which can cause us to misunderstand what the other person is actually saying.

An Egocentric Bias occurs when we embellish memories that make us look good. For example, in recalling our school grades, we might remember them being better than they actually were. This can cause confusion when we are reminiscing with someone who shares the memory that we are embellishing.

The Generation effect happens when we are better able to recall words that we have spoken, rather than the words of someone else. Clearly, this can cause communication distortions. Can you imagine the flow of this conversation?

The Next-in-line effect is when a person cannot remember the words of the person who spoke immediately before or after that individual. This might be because they are thinking about what they want to say. Then, they think about what they have just said.

Rosy retrospection is when we remember the past as being better than it actually was. Many family disagreements can begin as a result of this bias, when one person remembers a wonderful childhood, while the other remembers their shared childhood years quite differently.

A Self-Serving Bias involves favoring a situation or a point of view that allows us to look good or inflates our self-esteem. We might take ownership of situations that are favorable. If a situation casts us in an unfavorable light, we will tend to blame someone else. We have all done this at some point in our lives, especially as children. We are happy to accept the credit for getting an A on an exam. If we failed the test, we might immediately blame the teacher.

A Mood Congruent Memory Bias happens when we recall information or interpret memories that fit our current mood. Therefore, if we are in a bad mood, we can easily recall bad memories and interpret neutral memories as if they were negative.

The *Fundamental Attribution Error*, or the *Correspondence Bias*, is the inclination to assume that other people's behaviors are the result of personality flaws, while our own behaviors are attributable to situational factors. This also causes us to take benign comments personally or take offense easily.

The *Misinformation Effect* occurs when we witness an event or a situation, and later, others recall it differently. As a result, we become influenced by their misinterpretations and second-guess ourselves. We are persuaded by the recollections of others, and these influences can distort our own recollections.

NONVERBAL COMMUNICATION

Nonverbal communication includes all of the ways that we communicate without uttering a word. It's all about body language. Here are some examples of nonverbal communication:

BODY LANGUAGE

Multiple studies have shown that body language is more persuasive than the spoken word. Here's a simple example. If you are having a conversation, and that individual says "I completely agree with you," while shaking his head from left to right, indicating *"no,"* are you more inclined to believe his words or his body language (his head)?

Most would believe what his body language is saying – shaking his head from left to right. When words contradict our physical gestures, most of us believe the non-verbal clues rather than the spoken word.

POSTURE

Crossed arms or crossed legs indicate defensiveness or a lack of interest. If we are having a conversation, and the other person crosses their arms, this conveys a message that the individual is disagrees or is not interested in your words. In America, standing with your hands on your hips is seen as an empowering stance.

If we use our hands to emphasize the ideas we're expressing, our listeners will be more inclined to remember and ponder these ideas. Hand gestures are very powerful.

Slouching communicates insecurity, while standing up straight denotes a feeling of self-confidence an credibility.

EYE CONTACT

In America, making eye contact is considered positive, because it implies that one is confident and attentive. On the other hand, staring can be seen as rude. Eye contact is a very important in non-verbal communication, because it helps to increase the feeling of connection between the speaker and the listener.

FACIAL EXPRESSIONS

Think about how much information can be communicated with a smile or a frown. Even when communicating with those who speak a different language, facial expressions are universally understood. Smiling is very powerful because it helps listeners to feel comfortable and it eliminates defensiveness. Eye-rolling universally communicates annoyance or disbelief, and is considered rude. In the USA, winking can be interpreted as a flirtatious gesture, and sighing might denote boredom or tiredness.

TOUCH

Americans greet each other with a handshake, while French people kiss each other on both cheeks. I am an American of

Italian descent, and I can share that in Italian-American culture, women often greet men and women with a kiss on one cheek, while men usually shake hands with one another.

GESTURES

The thumbs-up gesture means, "Okay" or, "I agree", while snapping your fingers to get someone's attention, or pointing at someone, are both generally considered rude gestures in most cultures.

PHYSICAL SPACE (PROXEMICS)

The physical space that we create between ourselves and others is usually done on an unconscious level. There are four zones for different types of interactions: intimate, personal, social, and public. Most people are uncomfortable with close proximity, and preferring a comfortable social distance. If our proximity is 1.5-2.5 feet, we are entering the individual's personal space. This distance is usually reserved for people who know each other very well. Of course, with elevators, buses, subways or crowded city streets, all bets are off.

APPEARANCE

Appearance is very important, especially in work-related settings. First impressions are powerful, and people will often judge you according to how well you groom yourself, what type of clothing you wear, and, if you are a woman, how you wear your makeup. Our overall appearance is a form of nonverbal communication.

PARALANGUAGE

Paralanguage refers to the part of speech that includes accents, pitch, range, and volume. In the USA, loud voices are usually interpreted as an expression of anger. Being of Italian-American descent, I can assert that some people in my culture tend to speak loud, but this is not seen as offensive. What we (Italians) might view as an impassioned conversation, other might misinterpret as an argument.

NON-VERBAL COMMUNICATION

According to research conducted by Albert Mehrabian, words (what we say) constitute only 7% of our communication. Thirty-eight percent of communication occurs through para-verbal communication (how we say things, i.e., tone of voice, pauses, rhythm), and 55% occurs in non-verbal ways (expressions, actions, body movements).

PARA-VERBAL MESSAGES

Para-verbal communication accounts for 38% of communication, and refers to the way in which we say our words. This includes our tone and our choice of words. Do we sound angry, happy, sad, or forceful? Although we might try to conceal our mood, it is reflected in our communication. When we are angry, we usually speak louder, faster, and our voice changes to a higher pitch. If we feel defensive, our sentences are often shorter and more abrupt.

Para-verbal messages are easily misinterpreted, tainted further by accents, and which words we choose to emphasize. Here's a great example: Think about the sentence, "I owe you an apology." Now, read it with the emphasis on the words in italics:

- "*I* owe you an apology."
- "I owe *you* an apology."
- "I owe you an *apology?*"

Can you see how the emphasized word completely changes the meaning of the sentence? If I fold my arms or avoid eye contact, this adds to the confusion. The true message is usually hidden in what we do not articulate. Our posture, tone of voice, eyes, facial expressions, personal space, gestures, and even our silence, can speak volumes. Actions always speak louder than words!

RESENTMENTS CREATED DURING THE LAG TIME

Have you ever noticed that, when you are having a conversation, and the person is long-winded, your thoughts begin to drift? When this happens, you stop listening to the other person, as you begin to formulate your response, or your thoughts are simply elsewhere. You have completely lost your concentration.

The time it takes to articulate a message contributes to this gap. People can understand and process 600-1,000 words in a minute. Most of us speak about 175-200 words in one minute. The gap between what is said and what we hear, is linked to how slow or fast a person speaks. Because of this, our thoughts drift, we lose our focus, and we stop processing the message.

Competitive listening often happens when we don't agree with the speaker's comments, so we simply stop listening and tune them out. Here are some helpful tips:

- Try to be empathetic, by not judging what is being said. Statements can easily be misunderstood, when they differ from our own opinions.
- Don't interrupt while the person is still speaking. You can ask for clarification later.
- Try to respect their point of view, even if you disagree.

CLOSING THOUGHTS

I hope that this brief chapter has helped to explain how confusing even a simple conversation can be. When you think about the complexities and the many components involved with exchanging information with one another, it's amazing that we can communicate with each other on any level. Understanding this information can be helpful in eliminating some of the contamination in our communication, which might potentially lead to resentments.

16

RELATIONSHIP BOUNDARIES

*"We cannot control the behavior of others,
but we have complete control over
how we allow them to treat us."*

IMAGINE A WORLD WITHOUT RULES AND LAWS. It would be utter chaos. Likewise, our relationships can become disastrous if we fail to set clear boundaries. These are the limitations that express what we will and will not accept in our social interactions. Boundaries are important in helping us to prevent misunderstandings, conflicts, and resentments.

We all have physical and emotional boundaries that we express through our words and actions. Our physical boundaries include our personal space and our privacy. An intrusion of our physical boundaries can include unwelcome touch, someone standing too close to us, or any invasions of our privacy. Emotional boundaries are about our feelings and how we respond to various situations or particular words. Since people and relationships evolve, re-settings boundaries can be an ongoing process.

When we are offended, it is usually because we feel that our boundaries were disrespected, or we have not established clear and strong guidelines. Sometimes we only realize that our boundaries have been violated after a confrontation. If this happens, then we will need to reaffirm our boundaries.

Most of us have difficulty setting and maintaining healthy boundaries. We might feel uncomfortable asserting ourselves, or we struggle with saying "no". The fear of abandonment can contribute to these difficulties. If we don't set clear boundaries, however, we might have ongoing conflicts.

THE DIFFICULT NO WORD

Many individuals have trouble declining a request. Even the mere thought of saying *no* can trigger anxiety. Some people will say *yes,* even though they don't want to do what is asked of them. Then they develop a resentment, become angry with themselves, or feel taken advantage of by others. Nonetheless, we can't blame others if we aren't asserting ourselves.

In the past, I have struggled with setting clear boundaries. This was due, in part, because I didn't want disappoint others, or cause them to think badly of me. As a result, I felt angry with myself, and resentful toward the person who overstepped my boundaries. With time, I learned to be more assertive in expressing my limits, and this helped me to avoid those uncomfortable situations. It gets easier with practice.

Here are some suggestions that can help:
- Pause before agreeing.
- Don't feel guilty for asserting yourself.
- Respond to a request by saying that you will need to check your schedule and get back to them. This will give you time and help you to avoid responding impulsively.

VOCALLY ASSERTING OUR BOUNDARIES

If one of our boundaries has been violated, we need to tell the individual, so they will know that their actions were unacceptable. We can express ourselves politely and assertively. If others don't feel that they are being attacked, then they will be less inclined to take offense. If we choose our words carefully, we can avoid an argument.

Keep in mind that people cannot read our minds, and sometimes they can violate our boundaries without realizing this. If the person becomes combative, then exit the situation, and think about whether or not you want to remain in the relationship.

ESTABLISHING BOUNDARIES

Before you can establish boundaries, you will need to clarify what you consider to be inappropriate or offensive behavior. What makes you angry? What feels like disrespect?

What makes you feel that someone has taken advantage of you? Answering these questions will help you to determine your personal boundaries.

How do we express our boundaries in a non-aggressive manner? Here are some responses that are polite, yet assertive:

In Personal Situations

Strong boundaries are particularly important when dealing with those who are controlling, aggressive or manipulative. Here are some examples that can help in your personal life.

- "I can't..."
- "I don't want to..."
- "I choose not to..."
- " I'd rather not..."
- "I prefer not to..."
- "We obviously see the situation differently."
- "I need to think about it."
- " I am not able to..."
- "Please treat me with the same respect that I give you."
- "Please do not raise your voice when you speak to me."
- "I will not lend you money, so please don't ask me again."
- "Please don't use vulgar language."
- "Please don't gossip in front of me. It makes me feel uncomfortable."
- "Please don't take your anger out on me."

In Work-Related Situations

- "Please don't ask me to cover for you when you continue

to be late."
- "Please don't ask me to do your work. I have enough of my own work."
- "Please don't bring me into your arguments with other co-workers."
- "Please don't engage me in office gossip."

To Supervisors (If Possible)
- "Please don't reprimand me in front of others."
- "Please don't raise your voice."
- "Can we discuss this privately?"

When we don't feel compelled to abide by the restrictions imposed upon us by others, we can communicate more effectively. As we are more comfortable, we will develop more finesse in asserting ourselves. More importantly, asserting our boundaries will help us to avoid miscommunication that can lead to resentments.

BOUNDARIES AND BULLIES

Bullies are usually insecure people who want to be in control. Often, they were bullied themselves, so they try to protect themselves by overcompensating, and assuming an aggressive role. If they are obnoxious, they believe that no one will dare to bully them again. In overcompensating, they actually become the bully that they once detested. Bullies usually target individuals with weak boundaries, through intimidation and anger. Their tactics include raising their voices, criticizing, shaming, and speaking in a condescending manner.

Most of us have encountered bullies, especially during our childhoods. My bully was a girl named *Cecilia*. I will never forget her name, even though I was very young when this happened. Every day she would pass by my house as she returned home from school, and she would hit me and spew abusive comments. My mother told me that I needed to stand up to her. No one could do it for me. Well, one day I did just that, and Cecilia never bothered me again. Most of us have encountered a *Cecilia* at some point in our lives.

In efforts to keep the peace, you might have allowed yourself to be manipulated or controlled, or you might have apologized or agreed, to avoid a confrontation. In doing so, however, you have allowed the person to disrespect your boundaries and have given them the illusion that they were right. When we compromise our self-respect to maintain peace and avoid conflict, we are giving the bully the freedom to do and say whatever they want. Bullies do not stop. They will continue to test us, to see how far they can dominate us, until we set a strong boundary. If our boundaries continue to be ignored, then it is time to seriously consider exiting the relationship.

CLOSING THOUGHTS

We cannot control the behavior of others, but we do have control over how we allow them to treat us. If someone disrespects our boundaries, we have the responsibility to assertively tell that individual that their behavior was unacceptable. If it continues, then approach the closest exit, and detach with forgiveness. (Yes, we need to forgive obnoxious bullies too). Whatever our decision, it is important to protect ourselves and maintain our self-respect.

17

RELEASING RELATIONSHIPS

"Releasing toxic relationships is the highest form of self-respect."

IF SOMEONE CONTINUES TO VIOLATE OUR BOUNDARIES, then we need to consider whether or not this relationship is worth investing our time and energy. There are times when the only way to preserve our own sanity, is to walk away from an unhealthy relationship. The best thing that we can do is to save ourselves, and leave certain people in their own company. Nevertheless, it is important to exit these situations with forgiveness, so we are free from lingering resentments.

All unhealthy relationships have warning signs, but sometimes we might only recognize these in hindsight. Selfishness and self-centeredness are usually the most glaring alerts. The world consists of takers and givers. Those who are takers either do not have the capacity, or the desire to give. Regardless of how much we give to these people, they are never satisfied, and feel that it is never enough.

Takers will always demand more, and can become abusive or demeaning in their demands. These toxic individuals can be physically and emotionally draining. If we remain in these relationships, we will accumulate resentments, and lose our self-respect. Therefore, the healthiest decision we can make is to remove ourselves from these situations.

No one deserves to be in a relationship that feels like a prison sentence. You deserve to be respected, to be understood, and to be loved. If you are in a toxic relationship, you need to forgive that person and release them. This decision is more difficult and complicated when it includes family members. (Please refer to Chapters 9, 10, 11 and 12, for a more in-depth discussion on this topic.)

How do you know when is enough actually enough? Reflect upon these questions:

- Do you experience anxiety, at the thought of a particular person?
- Do you get a knot in your stomach?
- Do you experience anxiety?
- When you are talking to this individual, do your thoughts often drift elsewhere?
- Do you wish that you were somewhere – anywhere else?
- Do you pray that your phone would explode, so you can cut the phone call short?
- When on the phone, is it difficult to say, "Goodbye," or, "I have to go now", because this person will not stop talking?

If you find yourself wanting to escape when you are interacting with someone, these are all fairly good indications that your relationship doesn't feel like a beautiful day at the beach! Healthy relationships don't have us looking for the closest exit at the very thought of a particular individual. I used to play solitaire, when I was speaking to a particular person on the telephone. This individual would talk non-stop, and repeat the same stories ad nauseam. Eek! That was before I learned how to set clear boundaries.

If you are struggling to detach from a relationship, it might be helpful to write down some of the more glaring toxic elements. Is the person demanding, abrasive, judgmental, shaming, abusive? In what ways? Can you be happy and maintain self-respect if you remain in this relationship?

Toxic relationships create stress and chaos, and they can drain us emotionally. They are also fertile ground for resentments. If you have toxic people in your life, nothing that you say or do will change them, unless they have decided to change.

Expecting them to behave differently will only make you feel disappointed, angry and frustrated. In order to protect and take care of yourself, you will need to consider creating distance and limited contact, or completely departing from the relationship.

Unfortunately, certain people spend their lives blaming others for their misfortune, and seeing themselves as victims. If you challenge or disagree with this type of person, you can easily become their current scapegoat. These relationships can be very trying, and they usually do not end well. Forgive their offensive behavior, and don't set yourself up for more offenses that will require further forgiveness. Distance yourself from that person. If you try to sever ties with that individual without forgiving them, you will be left with the remnants of unfinished business and unresolved resentment.

As difficult as it is to depart from relationships, it can be far more difficult to remain in an unhealthy situation that frustrates and drains you. In severing ties with unhealthy people, you are taking away their power to create disruption in your life. When you have reached the point where the only option is to walk away, then you have affirmatively answered the question, "When is enough actually enough?"

We can spend years, or even lifetimes, in unhealthy relationships, because we feel that we do not have a choice. This is even more complicated when these relationships are with family members. We have been socially conditioned into believing that we have to make exceptions for family. We almost feel duty-bound to accept behavior that we would never tolerate from people who are not family members. Thus, severing family ties requires an enormous amount of strength and courage.

VALID REASONS TO LEAVE A RELATIONSHIP

- If the individual is physically, sexually, emotionally, or verbally abuse.

- When the relationship is based upon manipulation.
- When the individual is unpredictable.
- When the relationship causes ongoing anxiety.
- When there are ongoing, unresolved arguments.
- When the person is very judgmental or overly critical.
- When you feel that you need to constantly defend yourself.
- When the relationship creates chaos in your life.
- When you only hear from the person when they want something from you.
- When the individual is a taker, but never gives.
- When the relationship is only about borrowing or needing money.
- When the relationship is inundated with game playing.
- When you are being used as a scapegoat.
- When the person has an unresolved resentment toward you.
- If the person becomes angry whenever you disagree with them.

CLOSING THOUGHTS

Most of us know when a relationship is moving in a downhill direction. Sometimes we stay in unhealthy situations because we keep hoping that things will improve. It can take some time before we can muster up the courage to permanently let go. We need to be ready.

In detaching from unhealthy relationships, you are taking a monumental step towards protecting and taking care of yourself. It is nearly impossible to have self-respect when we allow ourselves to be disrespected by others. In leaving unhealthy or harmful relationships, you are taking a monumental step toward self-love. This is the highest form of self-respect. Without the negativity and the toxicity, you can reclaim your life and rebuild your self-worth.

18

MINDFULNESS EXERCISES AND MEDITATIONS

"It is my hope that you will capture a glimpse of the inner peace that lies within the eye of the storm – serenity at its very best."

LIKE THE TRANQUILITY WITHIN THE EYE OF THE STORM, there is a place deep within each of us that embraces the purest essence of serenity. It is accessible, but you will have to do some work to find it. Some feel that this place is where our soul or our life force lives. Maybe it is our spark of divinity, or our spiritual essence. Analyzing it is not important. Discovering it is a gift. After you walk through the steps of forgiveness, it is my hope that you will capture a glimpse of the inner peace that lies within the eye of the storm – serenity at its very best.

In my experience, this peaceful feeling is illuminated by a strong sense of hope. The belief that, regardless of our circumstances, everything will ultimately be alright. As my wise father-in-law would often say, "This too shall pass." I remember that I would be annoyed when he said this. That was a long time ago. It took many decades for me to truly *get* it. Unfortunately, I can be a slow learner. Better late than never.

In the worst of circumstances, during times of opposition, tribulation, and fear, I have learned how to access this tranquil place. This did not happen overnight. It took quite some time and persistent determination. Fervently, I have studied mindfulness and meditation. Study is the first level. These disciplines are not studied and achieved on an intellectual level. You have to practice and experience their power on a *heart and soul* level.

In hindsight, there are so many things that I could have learned from those who walked the path before me, and saved myself a great deal of grief. I guess that I was not ready to receive their wisdom at that moment in time. I hope that you might be more receptive than I was. The Buddha says, "When the student is ready, the teacher will appear." In my case, the teacher appeared and gave the message, but it took me a long time to receive it.

Inner peace was once an elusive concept. I had no idea how to go about attaining it, even though I desperately wanted it. I can see now that much of my turmoil was related to unresolved resentments, and this blocked my ability to experience inner tranquility.

I have been meditating for many years, and I find this practice healing and rejuvenating on so many levels. Once we begin to discover and embrace our center – our core of serenity – we will see people and situations very differently. Try to be patient with yourself. It takes time to evolve in meditation. Practice makes better.

The healing meditations and mindfulness practices cited in this chapter have been carefully scribed to assist you in creating a peaceful sanctuary within your heart, and ultimately, within your life. Gradually, as you evolve become comfortable with these exercises, you will begin to feel inner peace.

Mindfulness is different from meditation. As defined in this chapter, mindfulness is about paying attention to our present moment experiences and thoughts. We need to make a conscious effort to remain in the now. As we become more mindful, we are more able to recognize and overcome our resistance. Practicing mindfulness also allows us to recognize our negative self-talk, and how this influences our thoughts, moods and behavior.

Before you begin these exercises, feel free to create a calming ambiance. Light a candle or play some soothing music, if these help you to relax. For all meditations and mindfulness exercises, please find a quiet place where you can sit comfortably without being interrupted.

GUIDED RELAXATION MEDITATION

Allow your body to relax, as you sense this peaceful feeling extend throughout your entire body, from your head to your toes.

Now, feel the muscles relaxing around your forehead.

Feel your neck, your chest and your arms melting into relaxation.

Now, your stomach muscles are relaxing, your thighs and legs gradually following.

Become aware of the tingling in your toes as they begin to relax.

You are feeling very relaxed and calm right now.

Think back to a happy moment that you can recall. It might something as simple as looking at a beautiful butterfly, or sitting on a beach.

Maybe it was a song that filled your heart with joy.

Allow this feeling to create a sense of warmth and serenity within you.

Feel your heart smiling as you recall this beautiful memory.

Allow yourself to feel a sense of complete relaxation.

The following meditations have been designed to assist you further on your forgiveness journey:

SELF-FORGIVENESS MEDITATION #1

As you relax, gently become aware of your thoughts. Notice if any of your thoughts are judgmental. Recognize how interesting it is to see your mind at work.

Feel compassion toward yourself.

Did you notice many self-critical thoughts? Know that we all have these, and you are not alone.

Say, "I love you," to yourself.

Envision someone or something that brings joy to your heart.

It could be a person or an animal companion. It could be an activity that you enjoy.

Repeat these kind words to yourself:

May you feel safe and protected...

May you be joyful and peaceful...

May you be healthy and strong...

May you find inner peace...

May you learn how to love and accept yourself exactly as you are...

Envision yourself inhaling these kind words. Exhale any tension. Relax...

SELF-FORGIVENESS MEDITATION #2

Allow your thoughts and feelings to gently flow. See these as clouds floating by.

Feel your feelings without judging them.

Entertain the beautiful feeling of letting go, the deep, calming, inner peace that this will bring to your heart, your mind, and your body.

Take a deep breath. As you exhale, release any tension you might feel in your body.

Inhale peace, exhale anxiety...

Now, think of someone that you might have harmed. You need to forgive yourself and let go of the guilt.

Visualize this person. Say this person's name in your mind, and ask them to forgive you. Be open to receiving their forgiveness...

Hear them say, "I forgive you." Feel the surge of peace that begins to flow into your heart and throughout your body...

Allow yourself to experience the healing power of forgiveness...

Now, think about someone who might have harmed you, intentionally or unintentionally.

Bring forth a clear image of this person in your mind. Notice the feelings that arise when you think of this individual.

See this person as an imperfect human being, with their own story, and their own history. Offer that individual the same forgiveness that you wanted from the people you have harmed.

In your mind's eye, say their name, and say, *I forgive you*.

Now, watch that person gently floating away into the clouds...

Feel the sense of freedom and release...

Feel the cumbersome burden being lifted.

Take a deep breath ... as you exhale, feel the last bit of tension leave your body...

Continue this exercise, and envision others that you might be struggling to forgive.

Now, think of the ways you might have harmed yourself. Say your name, and say, "I forgive you."

Sometimes, we need to forgive a situation rather than a person. An example might be a health issue. In this case, bring forth the situation, and say, "I forgive you."

Now, congratulate yourself for a job well done...

When you are ready, return to the present moment.

RELAXING BESIDE A BEAUTIFUL POND (FORGIVENESS MEDITATION)

Begin by taking a few deep, relaxing breaths.

Once you feel centered, call upon any spiritual supporters that come to mind. These can be angels, spirit guides, loved ones in the afterlife, or just your own higher self. As you begin this meditation, know that you are safe and fully surrounded by love.

Imagine yourself sitting in front of a beautiful pond on a warm summer day. The sun is shining and you can feel its warmth on your face.

You hear birds chirping, and you feel a warm, gentle breeze.

With your spiritual supporters beside you, set your intention. You might say, "I am here to forgive all whom I need to forgive, so that I may be free to live my best life."

One of your spiritual supporters hands you a magical wand. Holding it, you feel relaxed and empowered.

Across the pond, you now see someone walking to the edge. As you continue to look, the image becomes clearer, and you realize that this is the first person you want to forgive. Keep breathing slowly, as you allow yourself to see this person fully.

The resentment has taken the physical form of a tube filled with darkness. This tube floats between the two of you. You can clearly see all of the darkness and negativity, between you and this other person.

Now, picture a cord that is extending from tube, and it is attached to you. Feel the sensation of how this cord is draining your energy and filling you with poison and toxins.

Look deeply into the other person's eyes and say, "I acknowledge that you (hurt, betrayed, angered, abused) me. I have been carrying this with me, and I am willing to release it completely. I forgive and release all patterns of negativity between us."

As you say these words, wave your wand, and watch the cord sever.

Say, "I am detached from you, and you are released from me. I am free and I set you free. There is nothing unfinished between us now, and all karma is fully healed and balanced in all directions of time. We are both free."

Before this person leaves, you begin to take a more empowering step. Put your hands together in front of your heart, slightly bow your head, say, "Thank you for teaching me to be more loving, kind, and compassionate towards myself and others."

Just the fact that you are willing to forgive, makes you a loving and kind person.

As the person bows to you and leaves, you notice the severed cord between you sinking into the pond. As the pond consumes the cord, it is transformed into a magnificent lotus flower. Symbolically, this lotus flower is you. You have risen above the murky waters of your experience with that person, and have emerged pure, beautiful, and unblemished.

Take a deep breath as you feel the freedom of letting go. Feel the lightness. Experience your mind, body, heart and spirit as beautiful as the lotus flower.

Now repeat this exercise with any other person that you need to forgive.

After you have forgiven everyone, thank yourself for taking this important step on your path of happiness.

As a final step, imagine yourself stepping into the beautiful pond, where it cleanses you of any remaining residue, and the lotus flowers permeate you with their healing energy.

Sit there quietly for a couple of minutes to center yourself. Drink some fresh water, or go for a nature walk.

Enjoy your newly found freedom…

19

OBSTACLE BUSTERS

"It is my hope that these ceremonies will help you to soften your heart, and replenish your soul…"

RITUALS ARE POWERFUL CEREMONIES that emphasize transitions and important occurrences in our lives. They can be very influential in helping us to overcome resistance and stalemates. This chapter contains rituals to assist you, if you are struggling to forgive yourself or others.

THE FLOWER FORGIVENESS CEREMONY

If you are having a particularly difficult time in forgiving someone on your list, then this step might be helpful to you. You will need a vase with a flower, and a photo of the person. If a photo is unavailable, envision a picture of the person near the vase. (The flower can be real or artificial.)

Each day for 30 days, look at the photo (or envision the person). Then tell that person that you would like them to have all of the good things in life that you would want for yourself.

SAMPLE SCRIPT:

Hello, (name). Today I am sending you light. I wish you health, happiness and serenity."

(Eek! Don't despair. It gets easier each day.)

At the end of the 30 days, write down how you feel. Was there a change in your feelings towards this individual? Has any of the grudge melted away?

DAILY SELF FORGIVENESS RITUAL

Since some of our emotional distress is the result of our negative self-criticisms, it is helpful develop a daily routine to de-program ourselves. This ritual is done in the morning, and before you go to sleep. You can do this while you're brushing your teeth in the morning, and when you're getting ready to retire for the evening. It takes less than a minute.

Daily, we need to let go of the luggage of self criticism. At first, this ritual will feel uncomfortable. We are not accustomed to saying comforting words to ourselves. Honestly, when have you ever said "I love you" to yourself. I'm guessing *never*.

Morning Ritual

Look in the mirror and say to yourself (out loud):
Good morning. I love you.
I am grateful to be blessed with this new day.
I have a choice to make this a good day.
I will take responsibility for all of my decisions.
I forgive you for any mistakes you might make.
I still love you.

Evening Ritual

(You can use a hand mirror.)
Look in the mirror and say to yourself (out loud):
I love you.
I'm sorry for any mistakes that I have made today.
I will try to do better tomorrow.
I forgive you.
I love you.
(Simple but powerful.)

FOUR-STEP SELF-FORGIVENESS RITUAL

Step #1: What is your story? Be honest about the stories you have been telling yourself. When you wake up in the morning, what is the first thought that pops into your mind. This will give you incredible insight into how you unconsciously see yourself.

Step #2: Envision yourself as you were as a fun-loving 6 year old. It might help you to find an old photo of yourself. Look into that child's eyes. Does the child seem lovable? Keep in mind that you are still that person at an older age. There was nothing wrong with you then, and there is nothing wrong with you now. You are still lovable and worthy of love.

How would this little child feel to know that she/he will grow up to criticize and dislike her/himself? To feel self-disappointment? Now feel the child's love for you – unconditional love and empathy.

Step #3: Look into a mirror. You are not your negative criticisms and self-talk. You are more than your faults and your fears. You are here for a reason and a greater purpose. You are here to learn and to teach. We all are. Try to embrace this truth.

Step #4: Jot down a few thoughts, as you reflect upon these questions:

What was it like to look into your eyes? Write down one good quality that you like about yourself. What do you feel when you think about your inner child or younger self? Make a commitment to be kinder to yourself.

Do this exercise daily for 30 days.

CLOSING THOUGHTS

Each morning upon awakening, you are presented with a clean slate and endless possibilities and choices. That's the great thing about life. Encourage yourself. Forgive yourself. Be your best *you* for today. Then repeat tomorrow.

You are here for a reason and a greater purpose, even if it is beyond your comprehension… Believe it…

In time, these ceremonies will help you to soften your heart, replenish your soul, and assist you in moving forward in your forgiveness journey. They have been very helpful to myself and others, and I hope that they resonate with you as well.

20

SEEKING FORGIVENESS FROM OTHERS

*"We need to say to ourselves,
'Okay, I make a mistake. Now I need to correct it.'"*

THIS CHAPTER WILL EXPLORE SITUATIONS where you were the offender rather than the offended, possibly causing others to hold resentments toward you. We are going to look at ourselves. (Doesn't this sound like fun?) We will also look at the benefits of developing an attitude of self-reflection and accountability, which will help you to recognize and rectify your mistakes quickly.

Unless you are another Mother Theresa (and I certainly am not), there will be times when you offend other people. Although you may not have intended to do so, it does not change the fact that you hurt another person. Depending upon the circumstances, you might owe that individual restitution as well as an apology.

It can be difficult and challenging to look at ourselves and acknowledge our imperfections. It is so much easier to be the offended person, because this is such a sympathetic role. As the offended party, we can revel in self-righteous indignation and gather allies. We can even have a pity-party, invite sympathetic guests, play sad music, and indulge in our favorite pain killers and emptiness fillers.

The role of the offender is not endearing: it comes with no allies, no sympathetic ears, and no pity-parties. Nevertheless, the fact of rectifying our errors has its own rewards and can be an opportunity for personal growth. We can make our amends with dignity and grace and learn from our mistakes.

When I was younger, I had a tendency to be short-tempered and impulsive. When I was angry, I would comment without thinking about the impact of my words, or the possible repercussions. The inability to control my anger and my words, got me into unnecessary trouble again and again.

I have worked very hard at learning how to control my temper and think before speaking, and I have gotten much better at pausing, and considering my words before I say them. Through unwavering practice, I have learned the delicate difference between reacting and responding. This has made my life much easier, and the number of people I have hurt has decreased considerably.

Like it or not, our character imperfections can get us into trouble. Here are a few questions to reflect upon. Answer honestly.

Do you insist upon getting the last word in an argument?

Do you feel a need to prove that you're right, at all costs?

When you become angry, is it nearly impossible to stop yourself from saying whatever comes to your mind?

Do you feel inadequate, if you don't win an argument?

Is it important to be right in every situation?

Most of us struggle with the situations presented in the questions above. Remember that we are imperfect, and mistakes don't make us bad people. We all have character flaws and, unfortunately, sometimes those flaws can cause harm to others. Our task is to correct our mistakes, and the first step is to acknowledge them. This takes some preparation work.

Our ego sees humility as the enemy. When we are in touch with our humility, we can see that pride and arrogance are not our friends. When we become angry, not caring about how our words might harm someone, it's usually our ego that is running the show. When we try to justify our right to attack or retaliate, our ego is cheering us on. When we act upon our anger at the expense of someone's feelings, we are, in fact, the offender in this situation.

To acknowledge our mistakes, we need to put aside our ego and be honest with ourselves. Unless we accept responsibility for our blunders, nothing will change. We need to say to ourselves, "Okay, I make a mistake. Now I need to correct it." This simple admission creates the path forward for personal growth. Like forgiveness, the desire to correct and rectify our error is a conscious decision.

Now that you are in the role of the offender, can you see how difficult it can be to apologize? It requires a disposition of humility to recognize our blunder, admit this, and rectify it. Although this might sound like a paradox, humility can be very empowering. When you look at yourself through the eyes of humility, you will be able to embrace the totality of who you are as a person. This action reflects a profound level of self-respect and a desire for personal growth.

Let's get started. Pen and paper at hand, write down the name(s) of those to whom you owe an apology. Who was harmed as a result of your behavior? Do you owe the person money, and need to include restitution as part of your apology?

In a situation where the offended party is deceased or inaccessible, you can make restitution through a donation in their memory. For example, if the person loved animals, you can make a donation to a local rescue, animal shelter or any organizations that helps animals. If you're unsure, donate to a charity for children or any other charitable cause. In a situation where contacting the individual would only open painful wounds, and possibly hurt them further, the donation option is a good Plan B.

I understand that it isn't always easy to apologize. In fact, sometimes it is just as difficult to apologize as it is to forgive certain people. Try to look at this from the other person's perspective. By offering an apology, you are giving this individual an opportunity to forgive you. This action can heal both you and the person you have offended. Like forgiveness, the ability to apologize marks a huge leap in personal growth. This opportunity takes us to the next level, since we are following through with our commitment to make things right.

CHOOSING THE RIGHT WORDS

Ownership and proper wording are vital when we are seeking forgiveness from others. Some apologies are ambiguous, and they are designed to avoid assuming responsibility. If you want to irritate the offended person, and make a bad situation even worse, here are a few gems:

- "I'm sorry that *you* were offended"
- "I'm sorry that *you feel* that way."
- "I'm sorry *you* misunderstood me."
- "I'm sorry that *you misinterpreted* my intentions."
- "I'm sorry that *you're* super-sensitive."

These words might seem like apologies, but they place the responsibility of the offense on the offended, rather than the offender. They lack ownership. In these examples, you are blaming the other person for reacting poorly to *your* offense. Not nice! If you are truly seeking forgiveness, then your apology needs to contain some essential components.

A compelling apology must contain these elements:

1. You understand and acknowledge *your* misdeed.
2. You know *why* it was hurtful, inappropriate, and wrong.
3. You feel regret and remorse.
4. You take responsibility for your inappropriate or hurtful behavior.

Don't blame the victim!

A good apology starts with, "I'm sorry that I said or did_____." or "Please forgive me for_____."

Here are some examples of sincere apologies:

"I'm sorry that I was rude to you. I was having a bad day and I took it out on you. I was wrong."

"I'm sorry that I borrowed money from you and never paid you back. Here's the money that I owe you."

"I shouldn't have blamed you when I couldn't find my keys. I'm very sorry."

"I'm sorry for judging you. Please forgive me."

There is a huge difference between, "I'm sorry that *your* feelings were hurt," and "I'm sorry that *I* hurt your feelings."

When you validate the person's feelings and express remorse, most individuals will accept your apology. The words, "I'm sorry," are healing. The words, "Please forgive me," are empowering *as well as* healing. They give the offended individual an opportunity to respond, and they reflect a great deal of humility. It is very difficult to remain angry, when someone humbly asks, "Please forgive me?"

What if the person refuses to accept your apology? This can happen. Just as we struggle to forgive some people and offenses, so do others. If the individual does not want to accept your apology, you have still done your part. You have swept your side of the street. You will need to accept their decision and move on.

If someone is not ready or able to forgive you, then there's nothing that you can say that will change their mind. Maybe they will be able to do so later. That's their journey, not yours. Walk away with grace and integrity, knowing that you have done everything within your power to rectify your error.

ONGOING ACCOUNTABILITY

By making restitution quickly, you will avoid an accumulation of baggage that gets heavier as time goes on. Immediately rectifying your mistakes will keep your life on a healthy forward path, free of debris and unnecessary headaches. Life is so much easier when we strive toward honesty, integrity, and ongoing self-improvement.

CLOSING THOUGHTS

We have come full circle in examining the various aspects of forgiveness from different points of view. Since we know that it's not always easy to forgive someone who has hurt us, we need to understand how others might feel that way toward us, if we have behaved poorly. I am hoping that the insights that you have learned in this book will help to soften the blow if someone cannot find it in their heart to forgive you right now.

If the individual accepts your apology, that's a gift. If the person is unable to do so right now, you will need to accept that too. Exit with renewed self-respect, knowing that you have taken the high road. (Consider giving that individual a copy of this book.)

21

EPILOGUE: CLOSING THOUGHTS

*"We cannot change the hurts that others have inflicted upon us,
But we do have the power to transcend our resentments
and transform ourselves."*

AS I WRITE THIS FINAL CHAPTER, the sun is beginning to set on a beautiful Spring day, and I am enjoying the moment that I am in. In the past, this simple pleasure was unavailable to me, because I was too busy ruminating about the past, nurturing my resentments, or worrying about the future. Now, as this book comes to a close, I am thinking about this path that you and I have walked together, and I want to thank you for allowing me the privilege of being a part of your forgiveness journey. I hope that, as you conclude this final chapter, a new chapter in you life will find you in a state of forgiveness, and open to all of the wonderful possibilities that this freedom has given you.

The Buddha said, "When the student is ready, then the teacher will appear." I hope that this book has been something of a teacher, and you were ready to receive its message. If not, please consider referring back to this book at a later time. You never know what the future has planned, and often, it can filled with surprises. As I have shared earlier, if anyone told me that, in the future, I would be writing a book about forgiveness, I never would have believed it. Yet, here I am, thousands of words and hours later.

My entire reason for writing this book is the hope that it might help someone else to move through and past their resentments, and afford them the opportunity for a happy life, free from the hurt of lingering resentments. I also hope that you can avoid some of the hell and lost time that I experienced because of my own struggles with forgiveness.

We all have our own story. No one else can understand the depth of your pain, because you were the person who had to live it. I can only encourage you to forgive, because it has changed my life, and I have seen forgiveness heal the hearts of others. I truly believe that forgiveness is the only solution for complete heart-healing and emotional recovery. Ultimately, however, it will be your decision.

When we have been betrayed, abused, or hurt by someone, we are left with the pain and the negative energy related to that experience. This energy lives within us in the form of anger, resentment and other unpleasant emotions. This energy also attracts negative life circumstances, creating a never-ending cycle of grief and disruption. Life is challenging enough without this added stress.

Forgiveness opens the doors to deeper levels of love, abundance and opportunity. It will also create new beginnings in your life. We cannot make room for the blessings of today and tomorrow, when we are still embracing the pain of yesterday. Although we cannot change the hurts that others have inflicted upon us, we do have the power to change their ensuing negative effects, by freeing our hearts, our minds, and our spirits, through forgiveness. You deserve to forgive, so *you* can be free and experience serenity.

After using all of the tools which I have shared with you, my life has been completely transformed. I have an inner peace that I never thought possible, and my ability to experience joy has increased considerably. I hope that you too have experienced some relief from your burdens, and you can smile and congratulate yourself for a well-earned accomplishment!

I know how arduous this journey can be. It is not easy – it requires determined effort as well as blood, sweat and tears. In 12-step recovery groups, there is the belief that, if we live by the tenets of the program, we will reach a level of growth, where we will no longer dread the past, because we will be able to use our prior experiences as learning lessons, and tools to help others. We are also promised the gifts of serenity and peace. In my experience, this also happens when we are able to forgive and move forward.

Many people have asked me how it feels when you have completely forgiven someone who has haunted your thoughts for years. I would like to answer this with a visual image. Do you remember the first scene in *The Sound of Music*, where Julie Andrews is singing the theme song, and she is dancing through the beautiful Swiss Alps? You can feel her joy! This is what total forgiveness feels like. Pure, magnificent joy!

Sometimes there are no adequate words to describe a particular feeling, and a visual image can often transcend words. If you have never seen this clip, I urge you access this particular scene on YouTube. This is the best explanation that I can offer on the feeling of freedom and joy that can be experienced through absolute forgiveness.

Forgiving particular people will probably be one of the most difficult, and yet one of most gratifying and life-transforming changes you can achieve in your life. You might need to repeat some of the steps, before you can fully forgive someone who has hurt you on a profound level. The deeper the hurt, the more challenging the work will be, and the greater the opportunity for growth.

I used to believe that life events happened indiscriminately. Happiness and adversity were distributed randomly, without rhyme or reason. After writing this book, and hearing the inspiring stories of others, I feel differently. I believe, with all of my heart, that there is a purpose for every single event and challenge that we encounter in our lives.

In hindsight, I realize that every experience in my life has broadened my insight, and has made me the woman that I am today. This is especially true concerning the struggles, the difficulties, and the challenges that I have encountered throughout my life.

Without the cloudy days we can't appreciate the sunshine. Without the obstacles, we cannot fully appreciate the moments that bring us joy. Without the struggles, we would not have had the opportunity or the motivation to get in touch with our strength. In fact, I think that our greatest wisdom is born when we overcome the struggles in our lives. Conquering adversity teaches us the some of the most valuable life lessons.

OFFENDERS OR TEACHERS?

Those who anger and offend us are often our greatest teachers. Sometimes we can experience a lifetime's worth of lessons from someone who has been a thorn in our side for years. These individuals reflect back to us our flaws – our limited capacity to love, our struggles to forgive – our anger and our fears. Ultimately, we are all in each other's lives to help one another to heal, love and grow.

In my acknowledgements, I conclude by thanking all of the unnamed and difficult people who have crossed my path. Although I did not realize this until years later, they have truly been my greatest teachers, by giving me the opportunity to forgive them, thus, contributing to my personal growth. I hope that perhaps you can view some of the difficult people that you have encountered with similar sentiments.

In closing, I want to share this final thought. I believe that the strength within each of us is greater than any obstacle in front of us. We just need to place our trust in this inner strength, and be willing to take a leap of faith. Clearly, since you have finished reading this this book, you have taken this leap. You have come this far, so I am convinced that you can successfully complete your forgiveness journey. We cannot change the hurts that others have inflicted upon us, but we do have the power to transcend our resentments and transform ourselves. And, that is my wish for you.

Just don't give up a minute before the miracle happens.

Wishing you serenity, love & light,
Nella

APPENDIX A

BIBLIOGRAPHY

Amen, Daniel (2008). Healing the Hardware of the Soul. New York: Free Press.

Boerma, C. (2007). Physiology of anger. Retrieved from http://healthmad.com/mental-health/physiology-of-anger

Enright, R.D. & Fitzgibbons, R. (2015). Forgiveness therapy. Washington, DC: APA Books.

Enright, R.D. https://internationalforgiveness.com/research.htm

Frankl, Viktor. (1959). Man's Search for Meaning. NY: Washington Square Press.

Frankl, Victor. (1988). The Will to Meaning: Foundations and Applications of Logotherapy. NY: Penguin Books.

Greer, S. & Morris, T. (1975). Psychological attributes of women who develop breast cancer: A controlled study. Journal of Psychosomatic Research, 19, 147-153.

Hendlin, Steven. (2004). Overcoming the Inheritance Taboo. How to Preserve Relationships and Transfer Possessions. NY: Penguin Books.

Hendricks, L., Bore, S., , Aslinia,D., & Morriss, G. (2013). The effects of anger on the brain and body. National Forum Journal of Counseling and Addiction, 2, 1-12.

Pattakos, Alex. (2004). Prisoners of Our Thoughts: Viktor Frankl's

Principles for Discovering Meaning in Life and Work. San Francisco, CA. Barrett-Koehler Publishers.

Pettingale, K.W., Greer, S., & Tee, D.E. (1977). Serum IgA and emotional expression in breast cancer patients. Psychosomatic Research, 21, 395-399.

Rosenfeld, Michael J. (2014). Couple Longevity in the Era of Same-Sex Marriage in the U.S. Journal of Marriage and Family, 76: 905-918.

Sood, Amit (2015). The Mayo Clinic Handbook for Happiness: A Four-Step Plan for Resilient Living. Boston, Mass. DaCapo Lifelong Books.

Thomas, S.P., Groer, M., Davis, M., Droppleman, P., Mozingo,J., & Pierce M. (2000), Anger and cancer: an analysis of the linkages. Cancer Nursing, 23, 344-349.

White, V.M., English, D.R., Coates, H., Lagerlund, M., Borland, R., et al. (2007). Is cancer risk associated with anger control and negative affect? Findings from a prospective cohort study. Psychosomatic Medicine, 69, 667-674.

Williamson, Marianne. (1996). A Return to Love: Reflections on the Principles of "A Course in Miracles". NY: HarperCollins Publishers.

Appendix B

Poetic Reflections

I have always been able to express myself by writing poetry, and the ability to do so has been cathartic and heart-healing. As I've shared in this book, I have experienced much challenge and adversity in my life. I also have ongoing medical issues. I see these as opportunities for learning and growth, and an avenue where I can share my experiences, strength and hope to help others.

Below are some of my poems that document different aspects of my journey. The first poem, *Forward Bound*, was written after I completed my forgiveness journey. The poem, *The Measure of a Life*, was written while I was in the process of writing this book. The other poetry was written during my younger years.

Forward Bound

I'm turning my back to the wind,
and waving goodbye to the should-have-beens.
Walking away from yesterday
and breathing the air of a fresh new day.

The days too quickly fly away
when we're too glued to yesterday.
The past has weighed me down too long.
Today I'm choosing a new song.

Walking with my head held high
my eyes are forward bound.
The past is gone. I'm moving on.
It's time to spread my wings and fly!

The sun has set on yesteryear.
I'm done with shedding rusty tears.
I see my life with fresh new eyes.
I've finally bid the past goodbye.

Walking with my head held high
my heart is forward bound.
The past is gone. I'm moving on.
as I spread my wings and fly!

The Measure of a Life

How do you measure,
The value of a life?
Count the moments of wisdom,
or the hours of strife?

How much coffee we drank?
How much love that we shared?
Through the lives that we've touched?
Or, the people who cared?

As the moments turned to days,
And the days turned to years.
Is our joy in our laughter,
or our wisdom in our tears?

Do we measure our growth,
in the miles that we traveled?
Is our wisdom the sum of,
the truths we've unraveled?

Then and Now, in Four Chapters

-1-

The deep colors of loneliness grasp me.
I am in a trance, suspended within time and space.
Solitude along can bring comfort,
Since it offers a pain free embrace.

Aloneness… nothingness… darkness…
These are my shades of solitude.
They cannot hurt me…

The words above were written years ago
by a little girl in pain,
trapped in the grasping clutches
of turmoil personified.

Young and powerless was she,
and although she tried to flee,
she was held captive
in camouflaged insanity.

-2-

Many years have passed since that sad time,
but search for self has placed me back
at the scene of the crime.

Standing face-to-face with a little girl within,
I need to give her a great big hug
and soothe her pain by trying to explain:

She was a helpless victim who was hurt,
and her beauty isn't marred
because of someone else's dirt.

The lonely, frightened girl who wrote this poem
was abused, hurt, felt unloved, and all alone.
She needs to know she's worthy to be loved.

Her solitude protected her.
Her poems helped her to cope.
She has the strength to survive.
So she can emerge and thrive
like the beautiful Phoenix
that is reborn… dusting off the ashes
so we can see
the precious gem
that lies beneath.

-3-

There were people in my past
Who have burned me with their fire of anger,
and slashed me with their scalpels of hatred…
Do the scars ever heal?

So the little girl of times gone by
only recently learned how to cry,
and found that numbing out the pain
will only allow it to remain.

She thought if she could just be a rock,
the hardness would keep the pain away.
And if she could be an island all alone,
sorrow and hurt would fall astray.
She was wrong...

-4-

And now, perhaps, still a child to some degree,
I wonder if the truth will really set me free,
since lies and denial only prolonged distress.
False armor and guarded aloneness,
didn't make the grief any less.

So, with stumbling fear,
like a child takes her first steps,
falls, gets scared, but then just tries again.

I will try to heal my wounds and then move on.

I will try to lock eyes
with the beauty that lies,
in the little girl within…

The Dark Years… A Little Girl's Tears

The colors of sadness
are green and pale brown.
Salty tears burn my heart.

The land of Oz is so far away,
And magic potions aren't real.

Sad realities consume me.
I feel like the weather today - dim and cloudy.
Or does the weather feel like me?

Lonely in a crowd, tasting solitude.
Cold shivers – hopeless tears,
Dormant fears…

I am in search of a new reality,
Far away from this prison.

Here I am Again

So here I am again.
Do struggles ever end?
Powerless once more,
Defeated by the score,
And frightened to the core.

The facts of life are bold,
Insensitive and cold.
They've clutched me by the throat,
forcing me to kneel.
They don't care what I feel!

So, if wisdom's born of struggle
does it ever really show?
When I finally find the answers,
Will I be the last to know?

Snapshots through Time

As the years spin in my mind,
Like snapshots on a carousel –
The twirling randomly stops,
allowing me to see
What was - what is
the total me.

Bits and pieces meshed together
Through the years,
Rusted by tears.
Cloudy thoughts now seem a hazy dream.
Did yesterday exist?

Happiness as fluid as the sand.
You hold it in your hand,
and it slides through your fingers so quickly,
that the experience is lost.

Caring too intensely.
Wanting more than they could give.
Can't let go of the need to hang on.
Not a healthy way to live.

There were those who have used
The knowledge of my weakness as a weapon -
A Sharp blade!
Deliberately inserting it into my heart
With compulsive conviction…
or so it seemed…
Giving them the intense thrill
Of watching my soul bleed to death.
And blaming me for telling the truth.
Verdict: Justifiable Homicide.

Lessons that I've learned so deeply
Have rendered me consumed with pain completely.
At that moment, feeling I would die,
But somehow I continued to survive.

But do I feel
more
or
less
alive?

Battle Wounds

I turn my back to the ominous wind,
and weep for should and could-have-beens.
Into turmoil I descend.
When will tasting anguish end?

And so, I'll go my lonely way,
Gnawing each minute of the day,
So weary from the uphill climb,
inhaling stress in double time.

Nightmares of the hornet's nest…
Mourning all the things I missed.
Is life, then, just an endless quest
in search for reasons to exist…

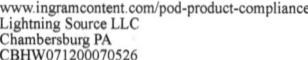